Master
the
Cast

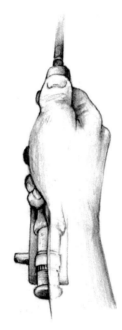

Master the Cast

Fly Casting in Seven Lessons

George V. Roberts Jr.

Ragged Mountain Press / McGraw-Hill

Camden, Maine · New York · Chicago · San Francisco · Lisbon · London · Madrid · Mexico City ·
Milan · New Delhi · San Juan · Seoul · Singapore · Sydney · Toronto

The McGraw·Hill Companies

1 2 3 4 5 6 7 8 9 10 DOC DOC 0 9 8 7 6 5

The Library of Congress has cataloged the cloth edition as follows:
Roberts, George V.
  Master the cast : fly casting in seven lessons / George V. Roberts, Jr.
     p.   cm.
Includes bibliographical references (p.   ) and index.
  ISBN 0-07-137972-X
  1. Fly casting. I. Title.
  SH454.2 .R63 2002
  799.1´24—dc21   2001008106

Paperback ISBN 0-07-144900-0

Questions regarding the content of this book should be addressed to
Ragged Mountain Press
P.O. Box 220
Camden, ME 04843
www.raggedmountainpress.com

Questions regarding the ordering of this book should be addressed to
The McGraw-Hill Companies
Customer Service Department
P.O. Box 547
Blacklick, OH 43004
Retail customers: 1-800-262-4729
Bookstores: 1-800-722-4726

Photographs by William Thuss.

Part-opening photo courtesy Nigel Calder.
Line art by Christopher Hoyt.

Contents

For
Marie Josephine Kippenberger
1919–1986

She would've thought it was neat
that her kid had published a book

Acknowledgments

Even a small book such as this is the result of a group effort. I therefore wish to acknowledge some of the people who have made this one possible.

Tom McCarthy, formerly of McGraw-Hill, encouraged me to pursue the idea when I was merely thinking aloud during one of our phone conversations, and he finally convinced me to make a formal commitment to the project. Ragged Mountain Press's technical reviewer added valuable comments to the manuscript. Molly Mulhern ushered this book through the editorial and production processes smoothly—or as smoothly as these things are likely to go. Other members of the editorial and production team I'd like to thank include Margaret Cook, Jonathan Eaton, Dan Kirchoff, and Deborah Oliver. Ragged Mountain Press published my first book, *A Fly-Fisher's Guide to Saltwater Naturals and Their Imitation*, and once again they've produced a better book than I could have hoped for.

My thanks to the photographer, Bill Thuss, whose keen trigger finger coaxed the shutter to fall on those moments when I look as if I actually know what I'm doing. Chris Hoyt, the illustrator, worked diligently to convey fly-casting concepts precisely, working from sketches and photographs, including those by Bill Hassan.

My thanks also to Penny Gentle, a serious student of fly-fishing, for taking part in the photo shoot to demonstrate both correct and incorrect technique.

My friend Sheila Hassan appears in a number of the casting sequences in the book. Sheila began as one of my casting students, and now teaches students of her own. Her million questions about every aspect of the game not only helped her to become an exceptional fly caster, but they forced me to become a better instructor. Sheila continues to teach me what can be accomplished through determination and hard work alone.

I cannot adequately express my thanks to Joan Wulff, whom I first met several years ago when I took one of her fly-casting instructors' courses—from which it took me about two months to recover. For the many people in this game who wish to be regarded as fly-casting authorities, I recommend you spend a weekend in the Catskills with this remarkable woman. If you don't come away with a profoundly deeper understanding of the discipline, as well as a new appreciation for the term "fly-casting authority," then you knew very little about the game to begin with.

Bill Chase of Angler Sport Group supplied the rods used for the photo shoot, and Tink Nelson of the Cortland Line Company supplied the fly lines. These two have been great about keeping me in new toys.

Most important, I wish to thank all of my fly-casting students. You've undoubtedly taught me more than I've taught you, and without you this book would not have been possible.

Master
the
Cast

Introduction

Fly casting is the most important skill in fly-fishing. It is perhaps the only skill you cannot do without. A successful fly-fisher need not know how to dress flies, tie knots, rig equipment, or even how to find fish. (You can hire a guide for that.) But a successful fly-fisher *must be able to present a fly to a fish.*

Despite the importance of the cast, the average fly-fisher gives less thought to it than to purchasing a pair of sunglasses. In fact, many maintain that fly-fishers need no casting instruction at all. And this is probably true for those willing to confine themselves to the easiest fisheries, where you can do almost everything wrong and still catch fish. But taking a dozen trout from a small stream doesn't mean you'll be able to take even one from a spring creek. Catching a thousand bluegills on a blind cast doesn't mean you'll be successful sight fishing for bonefish. Casting into a school of breaking striped bass is as different from presenting a fly to a cruising tarpon as shooting soda cans off a fence post is different from shooting skeet.

If you fly fish long enough and truly embrace the challenge, rather than the fantasy, of the game, you will eventually find yourself in a situation where the casting requirements exceed your abilities. Turning to your guide for direction at this point would be futile. For even if you were paired with the best casting instructor in the world, you would not develop the skills quickly enough to rise to the challenge of a difficult fishery in the space of a single afternoon—or even a full week. The skills of fly casting, like the skills of any physical game, must be built incrementally over time with practice. The time to concern yourself with learning to fly cast is the very first time you pick up the rod.

As surprising as it may seem, relatively few fly-fishers ever attempt to learn how to cast a fly rod—at least not in any formal or methodical way. Having myself spent nearly twenty years with a fly rod before I *began* to learn anything about casting, I believe you could spend a lifetime, without any form of instruction, and learn almost nothing. Your learning to fly cast in a vacuum well enough to perform adroitly in a difficult fishery is analogous to your learning to play the piano solely by ear well enough to play passable Mozart: perhaps one in 10,000 could do it.

Of those fly-fishers who do solicit casting instruction, only the rank beginner seeks to learn the fundamentals. Experienced fly-fishers tend to take a different view of things. Even with only a single season under his belt, the typical angler views himself as having somehow moved *beyond* the fundamentals of fly casting—whether or not he has ever been exposed to them. Without question, your having a firm grasp of the fundamentals is prerequisite to everything you'll ever learn to do with a fly rod. The angler who attempts to learn such techniques as hauling before she has refined such basic skills as loading the rod is like the basketball player who attempts to learn how to slam-dunk before she has become very good at dribbling the ball: each has put the cart before the horse, and neither will get very far.

I'm convinced that seven lessons can comprise all of the critical concepts and core skills of fly casting. Once you possess an intimate working knowledge of these fundamentals—as opposed to simply being acquainted with them—you will have laid a foundation that will bear the weight of all subsequent fly-casting skills. Once you have a truly solid grasp of the fundamentals, you will then be able to gain the command of the rod that you desire.

This book does not address the game of catching fish with a fly rod; many books in print already do that, some of them quite well. Nor does this book address the entirety of fly casting (a virtually inexhaustible subject). Instead, this book focuses on what I consider the most important aspect of learning to fly cast: building a solid basic stroke. My goal with this book is to help you build a solid, accurate, efficient, versatile, and dependable basic stroke, a stroke you can rely on to deliver your fly to its target consistently, under all conditions and in all fisheries, whether you fish farm ponds, lakes, rivers, surf, or tropical flats.

Master the Cast is divided into two parts. Part 1 presents an overview of fly-casting mechanics—both fly-rod mechanics and rod-arm mechanics.

Part 2 presents seven fly-casting lessons, beginning with the roll cast and ending with off-vertical casting from an open stance. Each lesson carefully builds on what you've learned in the previous lesson. I've also included an "advanced lesson" on hauling. Although this final chapter takes the book beyond the bounds of the fundamentals (and is arguably the least important part of the book in regard to developing a basic stroke), hauling is perhaps the most intriguing subject in all of fly casting, and no book would be complete without addressing it.

The appendix contains additional elements you will find useful in your fly-fishing education. The glossary collects all the terms that appear in boldface in the text, offering a concise definition for each, as well as a page number that directs you to the first full description of the term in text. You'll also find a list of books and videos that can help you build on your casting and fishing skills. Just before the index, the section on troubleshooting will point you right to the pages in the text dealing with solutions to common casting problems.

This could be construed as a beginner's book in that it assumes no previous fly-fishing or fly-casting experience. However, to dismiss this as a book intended only for beginners is to misunderstand it completely. For the concepts and techniques detailed in these lessons—and the depth at which they're examined—are of the utmost importance for all fly-fishers—beginner to advanced, freshwater or saltwater. No matter what you may think "advanced fly casting" entails, make no mistake: it is from the devilish details that make up the basic stroke that truly masterful fly casting emerges. No fly-fisher can hope to master the fly rod without first mastering the basic stroke. In some ways, no fly-fisher ever really moves beyond the fundamentals.

Just as all fly-casting authorities and instructors likely will agree with some of what I have written (for example, no authority I know of disputes the necessity of loading the rod), virtually all are certain to disagree on other points. Although I'm loath to proclaim that there is only one correct way to do anything, I'm convinced there are more, and less, efficient ways—more, and less, *accurate* ways—to execute a fly cast. This book does not propose to deal in theory; nor does it wax philosophic about such lofty and esoteric subjects as "the art of fly casting" (that tired expression). Rather, this book gives you a set of fly-casting mechanics that have been put to the test and have proved their worth on a wide variety of fisheries throughout the world. As a student of fly casting, you eventually must decide for yourself what you will, and will not, make a part of your game. And even if your game ultimately parts ways with the basic discipline detailed in this book, it still will have been an excellent place for you to have begun; for at the end of the day, all good fly casters are much more alike than they are different.

Realistically, nobody is going to learn how to cast a fly rod only by reading a book on the subject. Keeping that in mind, beginning fly-fishers can use this book to give themselves a solid background in the language, concepts, mechanics, and techniques of fly casting. Because it draws on the ideas of a number of fly-casting authorities, this book is a good introduction to the existing body of fly-casting literature. It is also a valuable supplement to good personal instruction and to fly-casting videos. Experienced fly-fishers can use this book to troubleshoot various parts of their cast and to help them reach a higher level of proficiency and understanding. Instructors of fly casting can gain insight into the problems most commonly faced by fly-casting students and use the book to structure their own lessons, clinics, or seminars. In short, there's something here for every fly-fisher.

A Word on Equipment

To begin to learn how to fly cast, I strongly recommend you use an 8½- or 9-foot rod that is balanced with a 5- or 6-weight floating weight-forward or triangle taper fly line. (If you wish to use a 5-weight rod and overline it by one size with a 6-weight line, this may help you in the early stages to better feel the rod load.) The fly line should be rigged with a 9-foot tapered monofilament leader, to the end of which is tied a small tuft of fluorescent package yarn. As you attempt the lawn-casting exercises in lesson 7, you may wish to use a bit heavier outfit, such as an 8- or 9-weight rod, which will allow you to handle a longer line a bit easier.

As you read this book, you'll note that I refrain from all other discussion about equipment, except where absolutely necessary. In general, too many fly-fishers devote too much attention to equipment; in particular, they devote needless attention to fly rods. Most of the fly rods on the market today are excellent casting tools, and virtually any rod on the market is good enough for you to use to develop the fundamentals.

For those curious, however, about the rods and lines we used for the casting sequences: For most of the shots we used a Marryat Packer, 8½-foot, 4-piece rod rated for a 5-weight line. The other rod we used (primarily for the long-cast sequences in lesson 7) was a Marryat Evolution, 9-foot, three-piece rod rated for an 8-weight line. I'm constantly being asked about what rods I prefer. The truth is, I believe there are many excellent rods on the market. Obviously I like the rods we used, and I think they worked well for what we wanted to show, but any number of rods would have worked just as well.

The line we used for both rods was the Cortland 333-HT, fluorescent yellow, which I chose primarily because of its contrast with the surroundings. To emphasize the loading of the rod in the photos, I lined the 5-weight rod with a 6-weight line (but in hindsight, I think this was unnecessary). I balanced the 8-weight rod with an 8-weight line.

Fly-Casting Mechanics

To become a good fly caster, it's critical that you possess a useful understanding of the mechanics of fly casting. In part 1, we take a close look at both **fly-rod mechanics** (how the fly rod and fly line interact to execute the cast) and **rod-arm mechanics** (how the various parts of your rod arm function to execute the cast). Having a sound understanding of fly-casting mechanics will enable you to gain command of the rod and line once you begin the actual lessons.

CHAPTER 1

Fly-Rod Mechanics

In most types of conventional fishing, such as spin fishing and bait casting, the angler uses a rod to cast a lure or bait that is attached to a very thin, light line. Because it has weight, the lure or bait could be thrown a good distance by hand, without the rod. In conventional fishing, you're essentially hurling a rock that's attached to a string.

In fly-fishing, the "lures" we cast—usually artificial insects and baitfish imitations—are made from bits of hair and feather and are virtually weightless. We could not throw them by hand. The weight we cast in fly-fishing is contained in the fly line itself; it is a long, flexible weight that unrolls through the air in an open-ended loop. The artificial fly is attached to the end of a tapered monofilament leader; the thick, butt end of the leader is attached to the tip of the fly line. The weightless fly is carried through the air by the energy of the unrolling loop.

The other major difference between fly-fishing and conventional fishing is that fly-fishing requires you to cast backward as well as forward. In fly-fishing, the basic cast requires a minimum of two casts to deliver the fly—a **back cast** and a **forward cast** (see next page, bottom)—as compared with conventional fishing, in which the lure is propelled on the forward stroke only. One of the great obstacles encountered by conventional anglers making the transition to fly-fishing is learning to cast backward.

In the basic fly cast, the fly rod describes an arc (see next page, top). This is not the simple V arc described by a metronome, however. Because the fly-caster moves his rod arm and hand to bring the rod through the stroke, the base of the arc is flat [_/]. Because of the rod's length, the tip of the rod moves a much greater distance during the stroke than does the butt of the rod. For our purposes, we can define the distance your rod hand moves during the cast as the **stroke length**, and we can define the distance the rod tip moves during the cast as the **casting arc**.

The basic fly cast describes an arc that has a flattened base. The base of the arc represents the distance the rod hand moves during the casting stroke, while the top of the arc represents the distance the rod tip moves during the stroke.

The basic fly cast requires a minimum of two strokes—both a back cast and a forward cast—to deliver the fly.

Loading and Unloading the Rod

The fly rod has been described a number of ways by various writers. Some writers have called the fly rod a *spring*. Others have called it a *lever*. Having no background in engineering or physics, I'm not sure what a fly rod is, in mechanical terms—nor do I think it's necessary to know to learn how to cast one.

The modern fly rod is a tapered graphite shaft; it is flexible and bends progressively from the tip downward during the casting stroke. It may help you, at certain times in your learning, to think of the fly rod as a spring, and at other times to think of it as a lever. However, the analogy I've found most useful to explain—and understand—the way a fly rod works is to describe it as being similar to a bow and arrow.

To shoot an arrow, the archer pulls the bowstring to draw the bow into a bend. Drawing the bow into a bend stores potential energy along the length of the bow. When the archer releases the bowstring, the bow springs back into position, and its energy is transferred into the arrow to propel it.

This is similar to the way a fly rod works. To cast the fly line, you must first pull the rod into a bend. Unlike the archer, however, the fly caster has no fixed point to draw against to bend the rod. To make the rod bend, you must pull against the weight and inertia of the fly line. This is called **loading the rod** (see illustration next page). Loading the rod stores potential energy along the length of the rod. To complete the cast, you must force the rod out of its bend by stopping it abruptly, which causes the energy stored in the bent rod to transfer into the fly line, propelling it either forward or backward. (In terms of fly-rod mechanics, the forward cast and the back cast are identical casts delivered in opposite directions.) Forcing the rod out of its bend is called **unloading the rod**. Without question, loading and unloading the rod together comprise the most important aspect of fly casting. Loading and unloading the rod properly is critical for distance casting: the amount of potential power you can put into any cast is determined by how deeply you can *load* the rod, and the amount of power you transfer from the loaded rod into the fly line is determined by how well you *unload* the rod.

Loading and unloading the rod is the most important aspect of fly casting, but it's also the most difficult to learn. Many fly-fishers never learn to load and unload the rod properly, or never do it as well as they might. The vast majority of fly-casting problems can ultimately be traced to difficulties with loading and unloading the rod.

Loading and unloading the rod—pulling the rod into a bend, and then stopping the rod abruptly to force it out of a bend—is a deceptively simple concept, so let's take a close look at it.

Whether it's lying on the ground or on the water, whether it's in a

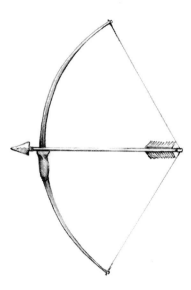

Drawing the bow into a bend stores potential energy in the bow.

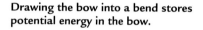
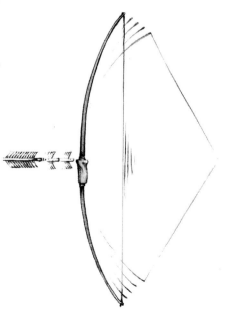

When you release the bowstring, the bow springs back into position, transferring its energy into the arrow to propel it.

straight line in the air behind you or in front of you, the fly line, for all intents and purposes, is at rest. Newton's law of inertia states that objects at rest tend to remain at rest; they resist our attempts to move them. When you use the rod to try to move the fly line, the inertia of the fly line resists. This resistance pulls the rod into a slight bend. Now you've started the fly line moving toward the rod tip. To continue to pull the rod into a bend, you have to continue to use the line's inertia and move the rod tip faster than the speed of the following fly line. To continue to load the rod, you must constantly move it faster: you must **accelerate** the rod tip over the entire casting arc.

Because the fly rod must accelerate continuously throughout the casting arc, many fly-fishers conclude that fast casting strokes are desirable. This misleading notion contributes to many casting problems, particularly with saltwater fly-fishers who are trying to add distance to their cast. Imagine a fly rod with 30 or so feet of line outside the rod tip. Imagine also that you could move this rod (through a vacuum) at a constant speed of 500 miles per hour. Because the rod and line are both traveling at the same speed, the rod will not

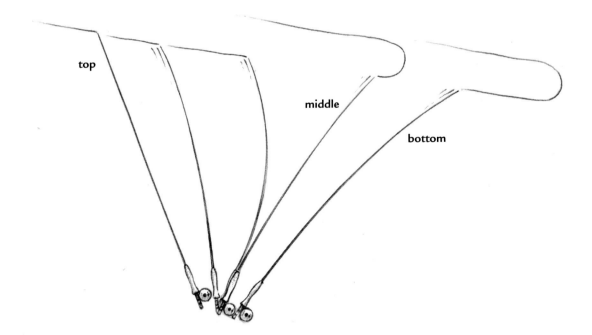

top

middle

bottom

"Top." The fly caster uses the weight and inertia of the fly line to pull the rod into a bend. This is called *loading the rod*. Loading the rod stores potential energy in the rod.

"Middle." Stopping the rod abruptly forces the rod out of its bend. The energy stored in the bent rod gets transferred into the fly line, propelling it forward (or backward, for a back cast). Forcing the rod out of its bend is called *unloading the rod*.

"Bottom." After the rod unloads, the airborne fly line continues to soar forward. When the fly line passes over the rod tip, a loop forms. Narrow or tight loops are desirable because they transfer energy more efficiently than wide loops.

bend. For the rod to bend, the rod tip must always be moving slightly faster than the following fly line. It's not speed itself that loads a rod, it's the gradual *increase* in speed: the acceleration. All good fly casts begin slowly. What's important is that they gradually, continually gain speed over the entire stroke. An efficient fly-casting stroke begins loading the rod as soon as the rod tip begins to move through the casting arc. At no time during the casting stroke should the rod move at a constant speed. To load the rod properly, you must accelerate it smoothly throughout the entire stroke.

Once you've loaded the rod, unloading it properly will ensure that you transfer all the energy from the bent rod into the fly line. The proper way to unload a fly rod is to stop the rod abruptly, which triggers the release of energy in the loaded rod: the rod tip springs forward (or backward, for a back cast), and the rod's energy is transferred into the fly line to propel it.

Affecting a **positive stop** is critical to unloading the rod properly. If you bring the rod to a gradual stop, the rod will begin unloading while you're slowing down. If the rod decelerates before coming to a stop, much of its power is lost.

Imagine an automobile traveling at 50 miles per hour. If the driver were to apply the brakes, the car would come to a gradual stop over a distance. Imagine this same automobile moving at a speed of 50 miles per hour and then hitting a brick wall. The car would stop dead, and every object in the car that wasn't fastened down would become a projectile. That's essentially what's happening when you unload the rod properly: the abrupt stop transforms the fly line into a projectile.

What makes the fly-casting stroke difficult to learn is that it's different from almost every other stroke you can imagine. A proper fly-casting stroke seems to go against common sense. When serving a tennis ball or driving a golf ball, you hit the ball hard and follow through with power. When pitching a fastball or throwing a javelin, you follow through with power. The fly-casting stroke is different from virtually every other sports stroke in that it concludes with an abrupt stop.

Many beginners (as well as many experienced fly-fishers) have trouble at this stage, I believe, because they envision the fly-casting stroke as a throw. They use the rod simply as an extension of their arm to "throw" fly line as they would throw a ball: following through with power. Even if they load the rod well, these fly-fishers sabotage their casts by failing to stop the rod abruptly to unload it properly. They bypass the rod's spring-flex action and simply hurl line forward and backward. If you bypass the rod this way, you might eventually be able to throw 40 or more feet of fly line—but it will never be effortless, graceful, or precise. In short, you'll never be able to "throw" line as well—or as far—as you can "cast" it.

All good fly casters, regardless of their "style" or "method," have learned to load and unload the fly rod properly. This is the foundation upon which all other fly-casting skills are built. As I've said, loading and unloading the rod is the single most difficult aspect of fly casting to learn. Once you learn it, however, everything else will be relatively easy.

Forming the Loop

As I explained in the previous section, a good casting stroke enacts a smooth, continuous acceleration and concludes with an abrupt stop. When the rod stops on the forward stroke and the rod unloads, the airborne fly line, which you've been pulling from behind you, continues to soar forward. The line is anchored at the rod tip, and when the following fly line passes over the rod tip, a loop forms (see illustration on page 10). The bottom leg of this loop remains anchored at the rod while the top leg continues to unroll forward.

To become a good fly caster you must learn how to form **tight loops**. A tight loop is the most efficient way to transfer the rod's en-

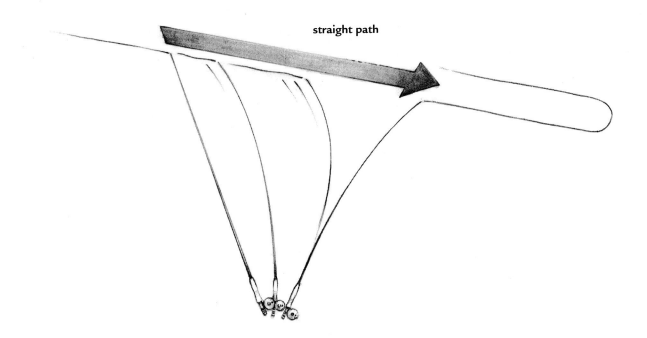

straight path

The cast will assume whatever shape the rod tip has traveled. If the rod tip moves along a straight path, the cast will assume a narrow or tight loop . . .

ergy toward the **target**, because a tight loop focuses all of the energy from the cast into a very narrow area. Forming a tight loop is critical to distance casting: the tighter the loop you can form, the farther and faster your cast will travel. Also, tight loops are less wind resistant than wide loops and are a must for casting into a wind.

The size of the loop is determined by the position of the rod tip relative to the path of the following fly line at the conclusion of the casting stroke. In a good fly cast, the rod unloads just beneath the path of the following fly line. The fly line that is anchored at the rod tip forms the bottom leg of the loop. The rod tip, when it recoils back into a straight position, is only several inches beneath the path of the following fly line—that is, the top leg of the loop. A good loop looks like a narrow U or V that has been tipped on its side.

If, at the end of the casting stroke, the distance between the rod tip and the path of the following fly line is significant, then the loop will be wide. **Wide loops** transfer power inefficiently; they don't travel as far, or nearly as fast, as narrow loops. Also, wide loops are more wind resist-ant than narrow loops and are ineffective when casting into the wind.

To form a tight loop you must accelerate the rod tip along a **straight-line path** throughout the casting arc, and then drop it only

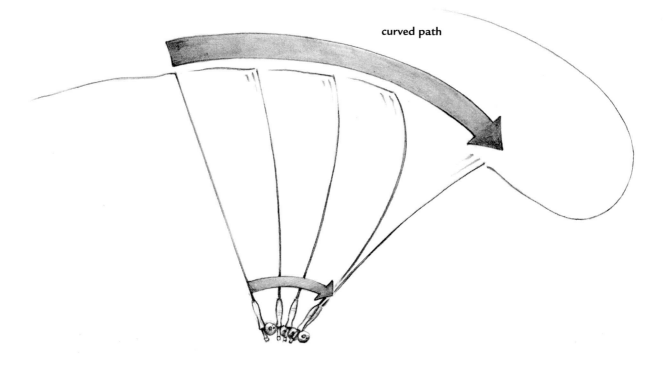

curved path

. . . but if the rod tip moves in a curved or convex path, the cast will assume a wide loop or nonloop.

slightly at the end of the stroke as you stop the rod to unload it. It's important to remember that the cast will assume whatever shape the rod tip has traveled. If the rod tip moves along a straight path, the cast will assume a narrow or tight loop. But if the rod tip moves in a curved or convex path, the cast will assume a wide loop or **nonloop** (see previous page).

As we've said, a good casting stroke begins slowly and accelerates smoothly. If you use too much speed at the beginning of the stroke, you'll shock the rod and destroy the cast. Very often a short, jerky casting stroke causes the rod tip to move in a concave path. This, in turn, causes the rod to unload above, rather than below, the path of the following fly line. This results in what's known as a **tailing loop** or **cross-loop**: the legs of the loop are crossed rather than open-ended. Tailing loops can tie knots in your leader (fly-fishers refer to these as **wind knots**, although they have nothing to do with the wind). In severe cases, tailing loops can also tie knots in your fly line. On short casts, tailing loops are most often caused by jerky casting stokes. Remember that on a good casting stroke the rod accelerates smoothly.

The loop of line is the single best piece of data to analyze your cast, for it always tells you exactly what the rod tip did during the casting stroke.

A short, jerky casting stroke often causes the rod tip to move in a concave path. When this happens, the rod will unload above, rather than below, the path of the following fly line. This causes what is known as a *tailing loop* or *cross-loop*; that is, the legs of the loop are crossed rather than open-ended. Tailing loops are responsible for so-called *wind knots* and, in severe cases, can even tie knots in your fly line.

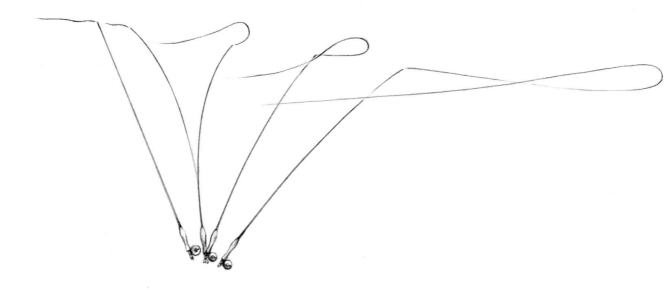

CHAPTER 2

Rod–Arm Mechanics

Until now we've spoken only of how the fly rod works and what it does during the cast. Now we must talk of what the rod arm does during the cast, for it's the rod arm's responsibility to make the fly rod operate properly.

In all situations, fly casters will stand or fall according to the proficiency of their rod arm. Graceful, effortless, precise fly casting is the result of a well-developed set of rod-arm mechanics. Awkward, laborious, inaccurate fly casting is the result of poor rod-arm mechanics. The vast majority of the casting problems I see ultimately can be attributed to poor rod-arm mechanics. All the principal gains you'll make as a fly caster—including gains in distance, power, and accuracy—will come through refining your rod-arm mechanics.

I may toss this out in only a few sentences, but I assure you these words are the summation of an education dearly paid for: your rod-arm mechanics will make—or break—your cast.

The Grip

There's nothing glamorous about the way an angler grips a fly rod, which is why, I believe, many fly-fishers forsake this early in their learning and simply hold the rod however feels comfortable or natural to them. However, the way you hold the rod is critical. Gripping the rod properly makes the most of your rod-arm mechanics, while a poor grip can effectively destroy your cast. Proper rod grip is particularly important for distance casting. Indeed, I'd guess that 90 or more percent of the students who come to me wanting to learn how to **double haul**—double hauling is considered glamorous—would add much more distance to their cast simply by learning to hold the rod properly than they would by learning to haul.

Although I have never played golf, I can appreciate the thoughtfulness and deliberation with which good golfers set their hands upon a club. How you grip the fly rod is at least as important to your casting stroke as a professional golfer's grip is to his swing. The average fly-fisher simply picks up a rod and begins waving it with little thought, if any, as to how the cork rests in his hand. When I conduct a casting lesson with an experienced fly-fisher, the first thing I do is ask to see his basic casting stroke, and then the first thing I look at is his grip, because that's the first place something can go wrong with his cast.

If you want to become a good fly caster, you must learn to set your hand upon the cork handle deliberately and properly, each and every time prior to the beginning of the cast.

For virtually all of my fishing, freshwater as well as salt, I use a single grip. It's known by several names. Mel Krieger calls it the **key grip** (that's how I'll refer to it in this book). Krieger also refers to it, in his popular book *The Essence of Flycasting*, as the **extended finger grip** (not to be confused with either of the grips we discuss in this section that use an extended forefinger).

The key grip is known by several other names. Joan Wulff identifies it as **Grip #1** in her book *Joan Wulff's Fly Casting Techniques*. Chico Fernandez, in his video titled *The Art of Fly Casting*, calls it the **handshake grip** (similar to the handshake grip in tennis). The key grip is nearly identical to the left-hand grip in golf.

To form the key grip, lay the rod handle across your hand at such an angle that the cork lies across the middle joint of your index finger and also across the base of your little finger.

Place your thumb on top of the rod handle so that it's in line with the spine or backbone of the rod (that is, in line with the feet of the guides on the opposite side of the rod). The pad of your thumb should be pressed against the cork, and your thumb should be flexed rather than lying flat against the cork. This puts your thumb in optimum "pushing" position, allowing you to load the rod well on the forward stroke. Placing your thumb flat against the cork, as so many fly-fishers do, will not afford you the same amount of "pushing" power as will the flexed thumb. Allowing your thumb to roll off to the side of the handle, or placing the tip of your thumb (rather than the pad) against the cork, both greatly diminish your ability to load the rod on the forward stroke.

The pad of your index finger should be directly opposite the pad of your thumb on the other side of the cork handle. The index finger gives you support to help load the rod well during the back-cast stroke. Whether I'm holding the slim, cigar-shaped handle of a delicate trout rod, or the beefy full-Wells grip of a saltwater rod, the handle rests in the crook of the first joint of my index finger (that is, the joint nearest my fingertip).

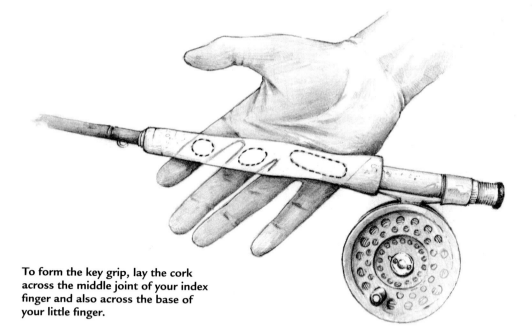

To form the key grip, lay the cork across the middle joint of your index finger and also across the base of your little finger.

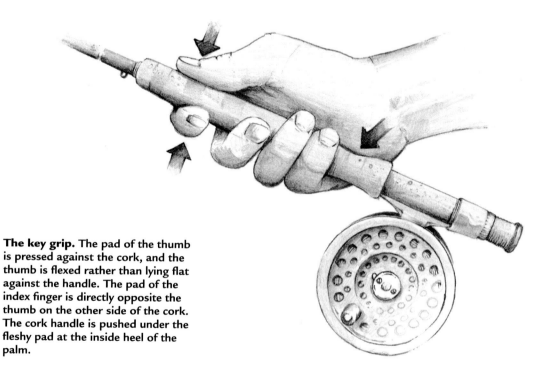

The key grip. The pad of the thumb is pressed against the cork, and the thumb is flexed rather than lying flat against the handle. The pad of the index finger is directly opposite the thumb on the other side of the cork. The cork handle is pushed under the fleshy pad at the inside heel of the palm.

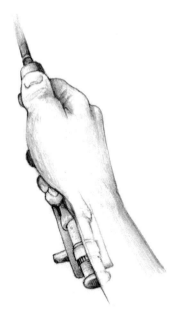

When you look directly down upon the thumbnail of your rod hand, nearly all of the rod butt should be hidden from view by your forearm.

The key grip holds the cork handle primarily between the thumb and index finger, as you would hold a key to turn it in a lock. This is virtually identical to how you would use your thumb and index finger to hold the handle of a screwdriver to put torque on a screw.

Two fairly common grips, both of which are much more popular with trout anglers than with saltwater fly-fishers, extend the forefinger along the rod handle. One grip places the index finger on top of the handle, directly in line with the spine or backbone of the rod, while the other lays the index finger along the side of the cork. Neither of these grips uses the index finger for support to load the rod during the back-cast stroke (which I believe becomes critical when trying to cast distance using heavier tackle), nor do they make full use of the hand's natural strength to load the rod during the forward stroke.

When you adopt the key grip, it's critical that the cork handle is pushed up under the fleshy pad at the inside heel of your palm. With the handle pushed up under the fleshy pad, I have the sensation that my hand is "on top of" the cork rather than simply wrapped around it.

When you grip the rod handle properly, the rod becomes an extension of your forearm, and the rod butt will be directly in line with the underside of your forearm. That is, when you look down upon the thumbnail of your rod hand, nearly all of the rod butt will be hidden from view by your forearm. Remember that the more abruptly you can stop the rod, the more of the rod's power gets transferred into the fly line. If you keep the rod butt in line with the underside of your forearm and push forward on the rod handle with the thumb of your rod hand as far as you can while pulling back on the cork with your lower fingers, you'll see that the structure of your hand, wrist, and forearm create a very solid arm-rod connection. This structure forces the rod butt, at the end of the forward stroke, to stop abruptly. Gripping the rod properly creates the strongest possible link for the arm-rod connection.

If you allow the rod handle to lie along the center of your palm at the base of your thumb (more or less along your lifeline), with the rod butt in full view as you look down upon the thumbnail of your rod hand, you'll notice that the rod butt can waggle a bit, even when you grip the handle tightly. The arm-rod link is not nearly as strong, which means you cannot stop the rod as abruptly as you can when you keep the rod butt in line with the underside of your forearm. One-eighth inch of movement at the butt of the rod may seem insignificant, but this distance will be magnified greatly at the rod tip. The rod will stop over a much greater distance, and you'll transfer less power from the loaded rod into the fly line. You'll never notice the effects of this on a 30- or even a 50-foot cast, but you will notice the negative effects on your longest casts.

Where you place your hand along the length of the cork handle is a matter of preference. In most cases I prefer to keep my hand near the top of the handle. Some fly-fishers prefer to place their hand closer to the reel. Particularly if you have a heavy reel, your outfit may balance better in your hand if you grip the handle fairly close to the reel. Also, gripping the handle close to the reel will, in effect, lengthen your rod by a few inches.

One word of caution about gripping the rod near the top of the handle: never place your hand so high on the handle that your thumb overhangs the crown of a full-Wells grip, or that it touches the graphite on a cigar-shaped grip or a half-Wells or western-style grip.

The tendency of many beginners is to clutch the handle in a death grip. This will fatigue your hand quickly and make a twenty-minute practice session seem like torture. For most of your casting stroke, you need only to grip the rod firmly enough to keep it from moving around in your hand as you cast. As we discuss later, the only time you need to grip the rod more firmly than this is when you squeeze the handle firmly and quickly at the end of the stroke to help you stop the rod abruptly.

Occasionally I'll see a fly-fisher who has formed the bad habit of gripping the rod handle so loosely that it actually rattles back and forth in his hand while he casts. That is, the pad of his thumb loses contact with the cork during the back cast, and his index finger loses contact with the cork during the forward cast. This is perhaps the weakest—and worst—of all possible grips.

I also see a good number of anglers who allow the rod handle to rotate in their hand during the casting sequence so that their thumb is no longer in line with the spine of the rod. This is equally bad. Once you've adopted your grip and begun to cast, the rod should not move in your hand; nor should any part of your hand lose contact with the grip, however briefly.

A number of students complain, initially, that the key grip feels unnatural to them. My stock answer to this is that fly casting is among the most unnatural of acts. The key grip might feel strange to you at first. However, if you spend only ten or fifteen minutes a day working with this grip—not only while you're casting, but anytime you get a moment to pick up the butt section of your rod—it will begin to feel much more comfortable and natural. As you progress as a fly caster, you'll come to understand the advantages this grip affords you in terms of strength, power, support, and control. In time, you'll wonder how you managed to cast any other way.

The Wrist

The wrist has two positions in fly casting: bent forward, and straight. The **bent-forward wrist position** is easy to find. Holding the rod

You achieve the bent-forward wrist position by pushing forward on the rod handle with your thumb while pulling back with your lower fingers. The bent-forward wrist aligns the butt of the rod parallel with the underside of your forearm.

handle with the key grip, simply push forward with your thumb as far as you can while pulling back with your lower fingers. Your wrist will naturally stop in the bent-forward position. The bent-forward wrist aligns the butt of the rod parallel with the underside of your forearm.

The **straight wrist position** is slightly more difficult to find, but only because there is no point at which you are forced to stop, as there is when you bend your wrist forward. The straight wrist positions the butt of the rod at a 45-degree angle to the underside of your forearm.

Each of your back casts will begin with your wrist in the bent-forward position (with the butt of the rod parallel with the underside of your forearm) and will end with your wrist in the straight position (with the butt of the rod at a 45-degree angle to the underside of your forearm). Each of your forward casts will begin with a straight wrist (butt of the rod at a 45-degree angle to the underside of your forearm) and will end with your wrist bent forward (butt of the rod parallel with the underside of your forearm).

Many beginners, and even many experienced casters, open their wrist beyond the straight position on the back cast; that is, they bring the rod butt out more than 45 degrees from the underside of their forearm—some to as many as 90 degrees. Much of the trouble casters have with forming tight loops on the back cast is because they "break" their wrist rather than simply straightening it. The rod butt should come out from the forearm to a maximum of 45 degrees. While learning to gain control of your wrist, you may find it helpful to focus not on "opening" your wrist during the latter stage of the back-cast stroke, but rather on simply "cracking" your wrist as you stop the rod abruptly.

Many beginning fly-fishers try to cast with wrist movement alone. Although you can make very short casts with only your wrist, you need to use your forearm and upper arm as well to make casts of even moderate distances.

In lessons 1 and 2 we explore fully the functions of the wrist in fly casting.

The Forearm and Upper Arm

If you were to cast using only your wrist, moving it between the bent-forward and straight positions, you could cast a very short line fairly well. With a 9-foot rod you could handle perhaps 10 feet of fly line, plus the leader, outside the rod tip.

To handle more than 10 feet of fly line outside the rod tip, you have to load the rod deeper. Think again of the bow and arrow. To shoot the arrow a very short distance, you need only to draw the bow slightly. But to shoot the arrow farther, you need to draw the bow deeper. It's the same with the fly rod. The bend you can put into the rod with wrist movement alone is sufficient to cast only 10 feet of line. But to cast a longer line requires a deeper load on the rod.

If you were to simply use more power to try to force the rod to bend deeper within the 45-degree wrist movement, you would shock the rod and destroy the cast. Indeed, many of the troubles I see with saltwater fly-fishers trying to gain distance involve trying to load the rod forcefully within a very narrow casting arc. Doing so will kill the cast every time and is responsible for countless tailing loops and "wind knots."

Remember that the rod must accelerate gradually and smoothly throughout the casting arc. To load the rod deeper without destroying the cast, you must widen the casting arc. If you were to try to do this by simply opening your wrist more than 45 degrees—that is, if you were to cast by "breaking" your wrist—you would move the rod tip through a large convex path and would be unable to form a tight loop. (Remember that to form a tight loop, the rod tip must move along a straight-line path throughout the casting arc.) To widen the casting arc while maintaining the straight-line path of the rod tip, you must use your entire rod arm.

The straight wrist positions the butt of the rod at a 45-degree angle to the underside of your forearm.

Opening the wrist beyond the straight position—here the caster has broken his wrist completely so that the rod butt is at a 90-degree angle to the underside of his forearm—will make it difficult, if not impossible, for you to form tight loops on the back cast.

To accommodate the straight-line path of the rod hand, you must use your entire arm: upper arm, forearm, and wrist.

To move the tip of the fly rod along a straight-line path throughout the casting arc, your rod hand must move along a straight-line path throughout the casting stroke. In its entirety, the fly-casting stroke is a compound movement: the back-and-forth movement of the wrist, within the back-and-forth movement of the forearm, within the up-and-down movement of the upper arm—a move within a move within a move. Used together, these three movements allow you to move your rod hand, and hence the rod tip, along a straight-line path. Learning to move your rod hand and rod tip in a straight line is so important to becoming a good fly caster that you should think of what you're doing as **straight-line fly casting**.

If you were to lock your upper arm in place and use only your forearm and wrist to execute the casting stroke—as many beginners are prone to do—your rod hand, and hence your rod tip, would have no choice but to move in a curved path, producing a poor loop. Incorporating your upper arm into the casting stroke—raising your elbow slightly during the back-cast stroke, and lowering it again during the forward stroke—is critical to your rod hand's maintaining a straight-line path throughout each stroke.

CHAPTER 3

The Closed Stance

The average fly-fisher probably gives even less thought to his stance than he does to his grip. However, proper stance is integral to good fly-casting mechanics and is responsible for balance, power, and accuracy.

There are two basic stances in fly casting: the **closed stance** and the **open stance** (we cover the latter in lesson 7). Throughout the first six lessons you'll cast from a closed stance. The primary requirement of a closed stance is that your shoulders remain square to the target throughout the casting sequence (rather than rotating sideways to the target, as they will when you cast from an open stance).

A good fly caster can cast well with both feet together, but I strongly suggest you begin with your feet shoulder width apart (measuring from the outside of your feet). Next, move the foot corresponding to your rod hand about half a step back, so that your toe is just behind the heel of your forward foot. Turn your rear foot outward slightly. Placing one foot behind the other will give you better balance and will also allow you to shift your weight to affect a slightly longer casting stroke (a wider casting arc) to make longer casts.

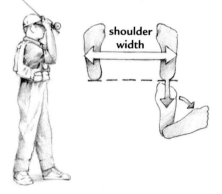

To place your feet properly, begin with your feet shoulder width apart (measuring from the outside of your feet). Next, move the foot corresponding to your rod hand about half a step back, so that your toe is just behind the heel of your forward foot. Turn your rear foot outward slightly.

The primary requirement of a closed stance is that your shoulders remain square to the target throughout the casting sequence.

PART 2

Lessons

The following seven lessons and the advanced lesson at the end contain the most important fly-casting concepts and techniques that you'll learn. In my ideal world, every student would be required to master each lesson completely before being allowed to move on to the next, and would be able to cast a long line without hauling before being allowed to learn how to haul. But that's simply unrealistic. However, I advise you to begin at the beginning, to spend a lot of time working on lessons 1 and 2, and to return to them frequently. Anyone who has truly mastered the roll cast and the pickup-and-lay-down cast can do virtually anything with a fly rod.

The Roll Cast

The **roll cast** is perhaps the most underutilized fly cast. It is highly functional, with numerous applications in both fresh and salt water, such as for taking the slack out of a fly line so you can make a back cast, or for lifting a sunken fly line from the water. The roll cast is also an excellent way to learn the mechanics of the forward cast, as it requires no back cast.

To execute a roll cast you must be on the water, as the water's surface tension **anchors** the end of the fly line, giving you the resistance you need to load the rod during the stroke. *You cannot roll cast on the lawn.* Conduct your roll-casting practice sessions at the edge of a pond with a fairly clean bank—don't stand amid bushes or tall grasses, which might catch the line and prevent you from making the cast.

Ideally, you should learn all casts on calm days. That's not always possible, however. If there is a significant wind, position yourself, if possible, so that it is at your back. Having the wind at your back will give you the least interference as you learn to roll cast. As a second option, position yourself so that the wind is coming in from the line-hand side of your body. The roll cast is difficult to learn with wind coming in either from the rod-arm side of your body or from directly in front of you.

Select a point on the water, about 35 feet away and directly in front of you, as your **target**. This might be a small clump of lily pads, a half-submerged log, a pocket in the side of a grass bed, or whatever. (You should always cast to a specific target, even if it's only a particular inch of water.) If you can't find a natural target, make one (from a bathtub toy, a Frisbee, a ring of foam pipe insulation, etc.). In any case, use a specific target and intend to deliver your fly to it. Assume the closed stance. That is, stand such that your shoulders are square to your target; your feet are shoulder width apart, and the

Roll Cast #1

Hold the rod tip low to the water and stroke it vigorously just above the surface to put a pile of line on the water next to you.

foot corresponding to your rod hand is half a step back and turned slightly outward (see page 23).

Strip about 20 feet of fly line off your reel and lay it on the ground on the line-hand side of your body. Grip the fly line loosely in your line hand. Next, hold the rod tip low to the water and begin stroking it vigorously just above the surface, to the rod-hand side of your body and in front of you. The water's surface tension will grab the fly line and pull it through the rod tip. Use fairly long strokes. Presently, all the fly line you've stripped from the reel will be lying in a pile on the water.

Trap the fly line under the middle finger of your rod hand and assume the key grip. (When you're casting while actually fishing, you ordinarily will not trap the line under the middle finger of your rod hand. Instead, you'll maintain tension on the line using your line hand—which we cover in lesson 3. However, it's best to learn the basic discipline using your rod arm alone.) Raise your rod hand so that your thumbnail is directly above your shoulder and is at forehead level. Your elbow should be pointed directly in front of you, directly at your target. The line of your shoulders and your upper arm should form a 90-degree angle.

Remember that you must begin every forward cast—and the roll cast is nothing more than a forward cast—with your wrist in the straight position, with the rod butt at a 45-degree angle to the underside of your forearm. This straight wrist will position the rod tip well behind your body. The fly line will hang from the rod tip and belly down toward the pile on the water. You may find it helpful in these early stages, as you prepare to roll cast, to think of a capital D: your body forms the standing part of the D, and the belly of line hanging behind you forms the curved part of the D. It's very important that the fly line hangs from the rod tip and bellies behind the rod

Roll Cast #2

Trap the fly line under the middle finger of your rod hand and assume the key grip.

Roll Cast #3

Raise your rod hand so that your thumbnail is directly above your shoulder and is at forehead level.

Roll Cast #4

The line of your shoulders and your upper arm should form a 90-degree angle, and your elbow should be pointed directly at your target.

Roll Cast #5

It may help you to think of a capital D: your body forms the standing part of the D, and the belly of line hanging behind you forms the curved part of the D. To load the rod properly for the roll cast, the fly line must hang behind the rod.

down to where it is anchored on the water. A common problem I see even among experienced fly-fishers is that they'll try to make the roll cast with the fly line hanging in front of the rod. To load the rod properly for the roll cast, *the fly line must hang behind the rod.*

It's virtually impossible to make a good roll cast in the vertical plane, with the rod tip pointed at the 12 o'clock position, as the fly line is almost certain to catch behind your rod, rod arm, head, or body on the forward stroke. Therefore, you must cant the rod outward slightly. To do this, keep your elbow positioned directly in front of you—your shoulders and upper arm are still forming a 90-degree angle—and simply tilt your forearm outward slightly so that the rod is pointed toward the 1 o'clock position (for a right-handed caster; 11 o'clock for a left-handed caster). If you keep your elbow positioned directly in front of you, with your shoulders and upper arm forming no larger than a 90-degree angle, the structure of your arm will not allow you to cant the rod any farther outward than the 1 o'clock position, as in photo 4 on the previous page.

Your pile of line is lying outside your rod hand. A right-handed caster must deliver the roll cast to the left of this pile, while a left-handed caster must deliver the roll cast to the right of the pile. If a right-handed caster were to try to make the cast to the right of the pile, the loop would cross itself and the line would tangle. This also holds true when the fly line is lying straight out on the water in front of you (as it is in the photo sequence). A right-handed caster must cast to the left of the line. Therefore, your target must lie somewhere between your pile of line and your line hand. If your target lies outside your line hand, you won't be able to form a good loop.

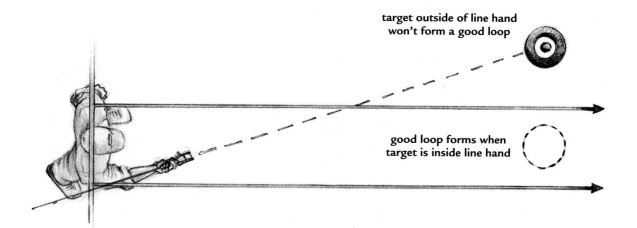

target outside of line hand
won't form a good loop

good loop forms when
target is inside line hand

Your target must not lie outside your line hand. If it does, you won't be able to form a good loop on the cast.

Let's recap as you prepare to make your first roll cast:

- You've picked a specific target, about 35 feet away, and you've positioned yourself such that your shoulders are square to this target.

- You have about 20 feet of fly line outside the rod tip lying in a pile in the water next to you; the pile lies outside your rod hand and in front of your body.

- You're holding the rod handle with the key grip, and the fly line is trapped under the middle finger of your rod hand.

- Your rod hand is raised such that your thumbnail is directly above your shoulder and at forehead level.

- The line of your shoulders and your upper arm form a 90-degree angle.

- Your wrist is in the straight position, with the rod butt at a 45-degree angle to the underside of your forearm; the rod tip is well behind your body.

- Your forearm is tilted outward slightly so that the rod is pointed toward the 1 o'clock position (for a right-handed caster; 11 o'-clock for a left-handed caster).

- The fly line hangs from the rod tip and bellies behind the rod down to where it is anchored on the water.

Look at your target, and imagine there is a straight line between your eye (that is closest to your rod hand) and the target. You can think of this as your **eye-target line**. Imagine also there is a straight line between your rod hand and the target. Think of this as the **hand-target line**.

Because your eye and your rod hand are very close together, the eye-target and hand-target lines run very close together as well. At your body, these lines are only as far apart as the distance between your rod hand and eye—perhaps only 12 inches or so. Imagine that these lines run toward each other gradually until they meet at a single point on the target.

These three lines—the eye-target line, the hand-target line, and the line that runs between your eye and rod hand—form what Joan Wulff calls the **accuracy triangle**. The narrower the triangle formed by the eye-target and hand-target lines (that is, the closer your rod hand is to your eye), the more accurate your casts will be—this holds true not only for the roll cast, but for all fly casts. Imagine trying to throw a dart accurately by holding the dart out to your side at arm's length. The same holds true for a fly cast.

During the casting stroke, your rod hand will move along the hand-target line. Again, I want you to think of what you're doing as **straight-line fly casting** (see page 22).

All good fly casts begin slowly, and so should you begin the roll cast slowly. Lead with your elbow. Your elbow should begin to drop and your rod hand should follow, moving downward along the hand-target line. The cast begins slowly and your rod hand continually gains speed as it moves; that is, your rod hand **accelerates** through the casting stroke. As your rod hand accelerates, the rod tip begins to pull against the fly line that is anchored on the water next to you. This begins to pull the rod into a bend: the rod begins to load.

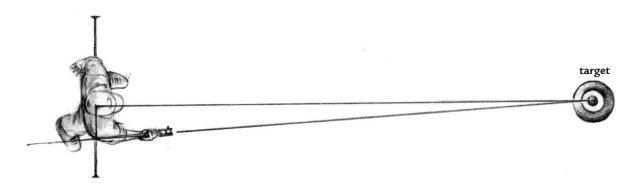

target

Together, the eye-target line and the hand-target line, and the line that runs between your eye and your rod hand form the accuracy triangle. The narrower this triangle, the more accurate your cast.

the hand-target line

You begin the roll cast slowly. Your elbow will begin to drop and your rod hand will follow, moving downward along the hand-target line.

Roll Cast #6

The rod tip begins to pull against the fly line that is anchored on the water next to you, and the rod begins to load. When the pad of your thumb and the butt section of the rod are about 90 degrees from the target, you'll push forward on the cork handle with your thumb as you pull back with your lower fingers.

When your rod hand has positioned the pad of your thumb and the graphite shaft just above the handle about 90 degrees from the target, you'll be very close to the end of the stroke. At this point, your rod hand will continue to accelerate straight along the hand-target line, and you'll quickly push forward on the cork handle with your thumb as you pull back with your lower fingers. This pushing-pulling action will move your wrist quickly to the bent-forward position (see pages 19–20). The structure of your hand, wrist, and forearm will force the rod to stop so that the butt of the rod is parallel with the underside of your forearm.

To stop the rod abruptly, your forearm must stop as well. To help affect the positive stop, quickly and firmly squeeze the cork handle as you enact the pushing-pulling movement.

The thumb of your rod hand functions as a sort of aiming device in fly casting. When your rod hand stops on the forward stroke, the line coming off the pad of your thumb should be pointed at the target.

Roll Cast #7

Roll Cast #8

Roll Cast #9

7. The thumb functions as a sort of aiming device in fly casting. When your rod hand stops on the forward stroke, the line coming off the pad of your thumb should be pointed at the target. 8. When the rod unloads, a loop of line will form and begin to unroll above the water toward the target. 9. As the loop of line unrolls, follow through by lowering your rod tip to the water. The leader should unroll the fly just above your target.

If you've done everything correctly, the rod will unload and a loop of line will form and begin to unroll above the water toward the target. After you've stopped the rod abruptly and the loop of line has begun to unroll, follow through by slowly lowering your rod tip to the water, directly in line with your target. As you do, your leader will straighten and your practice fly will lightly fall to the water very close to your target, if not actually touching it.

Although it takes several paragraphs to explain the mechanics, in real time the roll cast takes place within the blink of an eye: you start the casting stroke slowly, your rod hand accelerates, the rod stops abruptly, and while the loop of line is unrolling you follow through by dropping the rod tip to the water.

Troubleshooting the Roll Cast

We've just described a "textbook," or ideal, roll cast. However, it's unlikely that your first roll casts will be perfect. You'll almost certainly encounter one or more problems that will hinder your delivery. To become a good fly caster you must be able to recognize your mistakes and know how to correct them. So let's take a look at the classic roll-casting problems, as well as their remedies.

We've already touched on one of the problems with roll casting— catching your line around the rod tip, or your rod arm. This happens when you try to make the cast with the rod tip perfectly vertical. Remember that you have to cant the rod outward slightly when you make the cast. Imagine that you're at the center of a clock face, and 12 o'clock is directly above you. If you're a right-handed caster, cant the rod so the tip is pointed at about 1 o'clock (see photo 4). If you're a left-handed caster, cant the rod so the tip is pointed at the 11 o'clock position.

To keep the line from catching around the rod tip, set up for the roll cast with the rod already canted. That is, rather than lifting the rod vertically to the ready position and then canting it outward, make sure the rod is already canted when you lift it. This lessens the chance of the line tangling around the rod tip.

Even when the rod is canted, your elbow should be pointed at your target. Some casters have a tendency to let their elbows escape their sides as they set up for the cast. Beginning the roll cast with your rod hand a significant distance from your eye compromises both strength and accuracy, and you're almost sure to end up with some sort of a slice.

Many beginners try to set up for the roll cast by popping the fly line off the water. What this usually does is pull the fly line completely out of the water, and it ends up somewhere behind you. Remember that to make a good roll cast you need the end of the fly line anchored on the water. Set up for the roll cast slowly. After you raise the rod, come to a full stop and wait for the line to slide back and belly behind the rod to form the D loop (see photo 5).

A lot of fly-fishers try to make the roll cast with their rod hands at chest level. This greatly constricts the length of the stroke. This is extremely inefficient, and it's virtually impossible to make a good, accurate cast this way. Make sure your thumb is at forehead level when you begin the stroke (see photo 3).

If your line isn't turning over on the cast, it might be because you're not accelerating the rod through the stroke. Simply moving the rod through the stroke isn't going to do anything. To get the cast to lay out, you need to start slowly, speed up continually over the entire stroke, and stop the rod very abruptly at the end.

Many fly-fishers use a lot of force on the roll cast, and they do get the line to turn over, but it doesn't turn over crisply, or with any real power. Remember that it's the hard stop at the end of the cast that triggers the rod's spring-flex action and makes the line turn over. When the pad of your thumb and the shaft of graphite above the rod handle are 90 degrees from the target, you'll quickly push forward with your thumb and pull back with your lower fingers, and the structure of your hand, wrist, and forearm will stop the rod dead. It's this *abrupt stop*—and *not* how much force you use during the stroke—that gives the cast true power.

Remember that to form a tight loop, your rod tip must move in a straight-line path throughout the casting arc. In order to achieve this, your rod hand must move straight along the hand-target line throughout the roll-casting stroke, and it must stop on this line as well. If your rod hand veers off this line during the stroke, and your hand moves in a curved path, the rod tip will move in a curved path

If your rod hand moves in a curved path during the roll-casting stroke, the rod tip will move in a curved path as well, and this will be reflected in your cast as a large loop, also known as a **nonloop**.

as well, and this will be reflected in your cast as a large loop, also known as a **nonloop**.

This is why it's so important that you learn to use all the parts of your arm during any casting stroke—because a full-arm movement is the only way to make your rod hand move along a straight line. Pantomime the roll-casting stroke and you'll see that the only way you can make your rod hand follow a straight line is by using all the parts of your arm. Begin with your rod hand at about forehead level—where you'd actually begin a roll cast—and try to draw a straight line that slopes downward. You'll see that you need to lower your elbow as your rod hand comes forward. If you don't lower your elbow, if you keep your elbow stationary and try to hinge there, as many fly-fishers do, you'll have no choice but to draw a curved line. This is so important for you to learn: a full-arm movement is the only way to accommodate a straight-line path of your rod hand.

In a good roll cast, your rod hand moves along a straight line, stops on this line, and only after the loop has formed and the line is unrolling toward the target should you follow through with your rod tip down to the water. If you run the roll cast and follow-through together, you'll rip the loop open.

Remember that the roll cast begins the same as any forward cast—with your wrist in the straight position and the rod butt positioned at a 45-degree angle to the underside of your forearm. If you begin the cast with your wrist opened more than this, you'll drop the rod tip so low behind you that it will *have* to move in a curved path during the casting stroke, creating a large loop.

Some beginners break their wrists as they begin the roll-casting stroke; that is, they point the butt-cap of the rod at their target as their rod hand starts forward. This will kill your cast as well. Your wrist must never open beyond the straight position. That is, the butt of the rod is never at more than a 45-degree angle to the underside of your forearm. In the roll cast, the wrist stays in the straight position through the first part of the stroke.

Many beginners try to extend their rod arm fully on the roll-cast stroke. Not only is this unnecessary, it will destroy your cast every time. If you extend your rod arm completely on any forward stroke, the line coming off the pad of your thumb is going to be pointed down at the water at your feet rather than at the target. For a roll cast of this length, the necessary stroke is fairly short. At the end of the stroke, your rod arm will be bent significantly at the elbow. There's never any need to extend your rod arm fully. Again, remember that the cast will travel wherever the line coming off the pad of your thumb is pointed when you stop the rod. During a good roll cast, your rod hand follows along the hand-target line, stays on the hand-target line, and completes the stroke with the line coming off the pad of your thumb pointed at the target.

Your rod hand should never cut across the plane of your body on the roll-casting stroke. Instead, it should move directly to the target. If your rod hand crosses the plane of your body, you'll end up making a slice, and the loop you'll form, if any, will be poor. Remember that your cast will go wherever the line coming off the pad of your thumb is pointed when you stop the rod. If your fly line is having a tendency to lay out to the other side of your line hand, this doubtless is the problem.

These are the most common problems I see with roll casting, and if you're aware of them as you practice, your casting is sure to progress much more quickly.

Roll-Cast Variations

Ideally, you'll want to unroll the leader and fly just above the target, but there are times you'll want to make your cast actually unroll on the water. If you have to roll cast directly into a breeze, keep in mind that the wind speed is always slower close to the water. Unrolling your cast on the water lets you drive your cast under the wind.

To unroll your cast on the water, you'll still move your rod hand along a straight-line path during the casting stroke, but this straight-line path will be at a steeper angle. Rather than moving your rod hand straight to the target, you'll move straight to a point that's somewhere beneath the target, but still in the same vertical plane as the target. This causes the loop to unroll on the water rather than above it, and your leader is able to turn over with less wind resistance.

Once you learn to make a pick-up-and-lay-down cast, which we'll cover in lesson 2, you can use a **roll pick-up** to take the slack out of a fly line in order make a good back cast (see photos page 40). As

This steeper path of the rod hand causes the loop to unroll lower on the water.

To unroll your roll cast on the water, you'll move your rod hand to a point beneath the target. The straight-line path is at a steeper angle.

you'll see in lesson 2, it's impossible to make a good back cast if your fly line is lying on the water with a lot of slack in it.

To pick a slack line off the water, you'll make a roll cast that's aimed well above the target but still in line with the target. Your rod hand still follows a straight-line path, but it's a straight-line path that's angled upward (see photo 1 next page). Before the cast has unrolled completely, you'll begin your back-cast stroke (photo 2). When the back cast straightens, you'll execute your forward stroke to deliver the fly (photos 3 and 4).

The roll cast isn't simply a good learning tool; it's a highly functional cast for a variety of fishing situations. The better you can roll cast, the better an angler you'll be.

1. To execute a roll pick-up, make a roll cast that is aimed well above the target.
2. Before the cast unrolls completely, begin your back-cast stroke. 3 and 4. When the back cast straightens, you'll execute the forward stroke to deliver the fly.

The Pick-Up-and-Lay-Down Cast

The **pick-up-and-lay-down cast** forms the foundation of all straight-line fly casting. Virtually all fly-casting skills are rooted in this basic stroke. If you master the pick-up-and-lay-down cast, you'll be able to do just about anything with a fly rod.

In the pick-up-and-lay-down cast you'll lift the fly line off the water on the back cast, and then present the fly on the forward cast. Let's first take a close look at the elements of the pick-up-and-lay-down cast, and then we'll discuss the problems associated with it.

Begin with 12 feet of fly line outside the rod tip. With a 9-foot rod and a 9-foot leader, this will allow you to present the fly to a target 30 feet away. This is more than adequate to fish successfully in many freshwater situations.

Prepare to make the pick-up-and-lay-down cast by first using the roll cast to straighten your line out. That is, hook the fly line under the middle finger of your rod hand and roll cast the line straight to your target (see lesson 1). (Again, while fishing you wouldn't ordinarily cast with your fly line trapped under your middle finger. But we're still focusing on learning good rod-arm mechanics, and this is much easier to do at this point without involving the line hand.) Follow through with the rod tip down to the water. The fly line should be straight out in front of you with no slack, and there should be no slack between your rod tip and the water.

Every back cast begins with your wrist in the bent-forward position. Push forward on the rod handle with your thumb as you pull back with your lower fingers so that the butt of the rod is parallel with the underside of your forearm. Now you're ready to make your first pick-up-and-lay-down cast (see photo 1).

The fly-casting stroke is a continuous acceleration that concludes with an abrupt stop. Most fly-casting authorities describe the casting stroke as having two parts, or stages, within the overall acceleration.

Getting Hit with the Fly

Many fly-fishers are reluctant to cast in the vertical plane for fear they will get hit with the fly. The truth is that you're occasionally going to get hit with the fly, no matter what plane you cast in. This is why it's so important to always wear eye protection, and to fish with barbless hooks.

Because the fly line passes directly over your body, you probably run a slightly greater risk of getting hit with the fly when casting in the vertical plane. A slight error in timing can cause the fly line to fall, and when this happens the fly is more likely to hit you as it passes. Practice will remedy this. These days I get hit about as seldom casting vertically as I do casting off-vertically. So seldom, in fact, that it's no longer a consideration.

The first stage of the acceleration serves to get the rod, line, leader, and fly moving as a unit and begins the bending or loading of the rod. This first stage of the acceleration is known as the **loading move**. The second, or final, stage of the acceleration completes the loading of the rod, and then stops the rod abruptly to unload it. Joan Wulff calls this final part of the acceleration the **power snap** (that's the term used in this book). It's also called the **speed-up-and-stop**, the **power stroke**, and several other terms by various fly-casting authorities (but see page 52 regarding the limitations of these terms).

You can see the two stages of the acceleration most distinctly when making a back cast from the water. Begin the back-cast stroke by raising your upper arm and forearm to raise the rod tip to lift the fly line from the water. When lifting line off the water you must begin slowly and speed up very gradually during the lift to overcome the water's surface tension without making a major disturbance that might spook any fish in the area. The fly line is anchored to the water by surface tension, and the line you've lifted is, in effect, stretched between the rod tip and the **anchor point** (which shortens progressively as you lift line). This anchor allows the weight of the fly line that you've lifted to begin to pull the rod into a bend. The more line you lift, the more of the line's weight pulls on the rod tip, and the more you load the rod. As we've said, this first part of the stroke is called the *loading move*. The loading move continues until you've lifted the fly line to the line-leader connection (that is, the tip of the fly line). Once you've lifted the fly line to the line-leader connection, the loading move is complete. This line-leader connection is a critical visual cue to your making a good cast, and you need to pay attention to it every time you lift a fly line from the water.

As you lift the fly line from the water, you should concentrate on feeling the weight and resistance (inertia) of the fly line pulling the rod tip into a bend. Indeed, you should concentrate on this feeling during every fly-casting stroke. Without question, *your ability to feel the fly line pulling the rod into a bend is the most important feeling you'll ever develop as a fly caster.*

Once you've lifted the fly line to the line-leader connection, you're ready to execute the second part of the stroke—that is, the *power snap*. Your rod hand will continue through the casting stroke on its straight-line path, and your wrist will move very quickly from bent forward to straight; that is, the rod butt will jump out from the underside of your forearm at a 45-degree angle.

Keep your eye on the yarn fly. Like the line-leader connection, the yarn fly is a critical visual cue for the pick-up-and-lay-down cast. The instant this fly leaves the water, the back-cast stroke ends; that is, you must stop everything abruptly: your forearm, your rod hand, the rod—everything stops dead. To help effect this **positive stop**, you'll squeeze the rod handle as you end the stroke—very firmly and very

Pick-Up-and-Lay-Down Cast #1

Pick-Up-and-Lay-Down Cast #2

Pick-Up-and-Lay-Down Cast #3

1. Every back cast begins with your wrist in the bent-forward position with the rod tip at the water and with all the slack removed from the fly line. 2. When you lift fly line from the water, the weight of the fly line stretched between the rod tip and the anchor point begins to bend or load the rod. 3. Once you've lifted the fly line to the line-leader connection (out of view), the loading move is complete.

Pick-Up-and-Lay-Down Cast #4

Pick-Up-and-Lay-Down Cast #5

During the power-snap portion of the stroke, your rod hand continues along its straight-line path. Your wrist moves very quickly from bent-forward to straight. The instant you see the fly leave the water, you stop everything abruptly.

This positive stop triggers the spring-flex action of the rod and causes it to unload on the back cast.

quickly. This abrupt stop triggers the spring-flex action of the rod and causes it to unload on the back cast. As soon as the rod unloads you can relax your grip on the rod handle once more.

When your rod hand stops on the back cast and the rod unloads, the fly line will begin unrolling behind you in an open-ended loop. The instant the fly line straightens on the back cast, you'll begin your forward stroke.

From a closed stance, with your shoulders square to the target, you're not going to be able to watch your back cast unroll, so you're going to have to time this by feel.

As your back cast unrolls, you'll feel the weight of the fly line against the rod tip, increasing gradually until the line straightens completely, which you'll feel as a slight tug on the rod tip. The feeling of the weight of the fly line against the rod tip is subtle. It becomes more noticeable as your casting stroke improves, but it's always fairly subtle. If you're having trouble feeling the fly line as it straightens behind you, here's another way to time your forward stroke: When your rod unloads on the back cast, there'll be a shock in the rod. When this shock dissipates, begin your forward stroke.

On the forward cast you don't have the water's surface tension to overcome. So the first part of the stroke, the loading move, is going

Pick-Up-and-Lay-Down Cast #6

When the rod unloads, the fly line will begin unrolling behind you in an open-ended loop.

Pick-Up-and-Lay-Down Cast #7

The instant the fly line straightens on the back cast, you'll begin your forward stroke.

Pick-Up-and-Lay-Down Cast #8

The loading move on the forward stroke is relatively short, perhaps only a few inches.

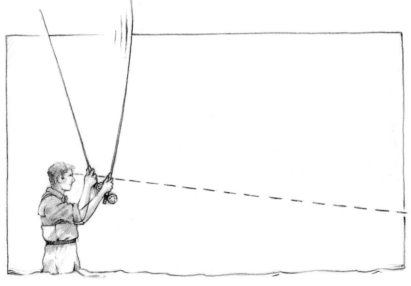

During the forward stroke, your rod hand moves straight along the hand-target line.

to be relatively short, perhaps only a few inches. During the loading move your wrist will remain in the straight position.

Envision the forward stroke as a pulling motion: you're pulling line from behind you, pulling the rod into a bend. Remember that on the forward stroke, just as with the roll cast, there's a straight line between your rod hand and the target. During the forward stroke, your rod hand is going to move straight along this hand-target line.

When you've moved your rod hand far enough through the forward stroke that the pad of your thumb (and the shaft of the rod just above the cork) is about 90 degrees from your target, you can execute the second part of the stroke, the power snap.

During the power-snap portion of the stroke, your rod hand continues forward along the hand-target line. You'll push forward with

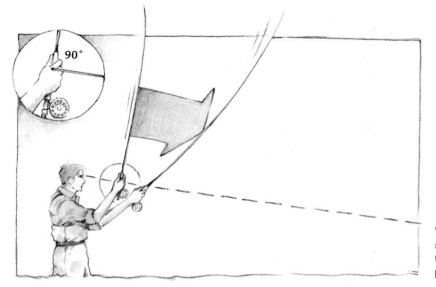

When the pad of your thumb and the shaft of the rod are about 90 degrees from your target, you'll begin the power snap.

Pick-Up-and-Lay-Down Cast #9

On the power snap, you'll push forward with your thumb as you pull back with your lower fingers. You'll squeeze the rod handle very firmly and very quickly, and you'll stop the rod abruptly. When you stop the rod, the imaginary line coming off the pad of your thumb will be pointed at the target.

your thumb as you pull back with your lower fingers. As you do this, you'll squeeze the rod handle very firmly and very quickly, and you'll stop the rod abruptly. When you stop the rod, the imaginary line coming off the pad of your thumb will be pointed at the target.

What helped me to best understand the mechanics of the power snap is Joan Wulff's analogy of the screen-door handle. To open a screen door you push forward on the button with your thumb as you pull back on the handle with your lower fingers. At the conclusion of the power snap, the structure of your hand and wrist cause the rod to stop abruptly, with the rod butt parallel to the underside of your forearm.

When the rod stops abruptly, the rod will unload just beneath the path of following fly line. A loop will form, and the line, leader, and

Pick-Up-and-Lay-Down Cast #10

Pick-Up-and-Lay-Down Cast #11

10. When the rod stops abruptly, the rod will unload just beneath the path of following fly line. A loop will form, and the line, leader, and fly will begin to unroll toward the target. 11. As the loop is unrolling, you'll follow through with the rod tip down to the water.

fly will begin to unroll toward the target. As the loop is unrolling, you'll follow through with the rod tip down to the water. Finishing the cast with your rod tip down at the water puts you in good position to fish (because you're automatically tight to the fly) and also puts you in good position to make another cast.

When you first begin to fly cast, there's a tremendous amount of information you have to keep in your head. Try not to let it overwhelm you, and don't let it discourage you. Spend some time working with the rod, and fly casting will become every bit as easy as good casters make it look.

Common Mistakes

We've just gone through our ideal pick-up-and-lay-down cast. However, chances are that you're not going to get it perfect the first time, so let's review some of the most common mistakes.

The first problems any fly-fisher is likely to encounter with the pick-up-and-lay-down cast will involve lifting the fly line from the water. Many casters tend to begin their back-cast stroke with their rod tip several feet above the water. In fact, this is perhaps the most common mistake throughout all of fly casting, and it should be addressed as soon as possible in the fly-fisher's education. Beginning the back-cast stroke with the rod tip above the water is extremely inefficient; for if you begin the back cast with the rod tip, say, 3 feet above the water's surface, what you've actually done, in effect, is insert 3 feet of slack into your cast and eliminate 3 feet from your casting arc. With a short line, you'll still be able to make the cast. But if you have any appreciable amount of fly line outside the rod tip, you won't be able to make a good back cast. In fly casting—and in distance fly casting in particular—you cannot overestimate the importance of the back cast: *if you've got no back cast, then you've got no cast.* Begin every pick-up-and-lay-down cast with the rod tip touching the water and every inch of slack removed from the fly line (see photo 1).

Most fly-fishers, when they first attempt to learn the pick-up-and-lay-down cast, try to lift the fly line off the water with too much speed or force, which will rip the line off the water. You'll actually hear the line rip, and you'll see the line of white spray it creates (the British call this the *white mouse*). When you're trout fishing, ripping the fly line off the water will likely spook any fish in the area.

Conversely, if you lift the line too slowly during the first part of the acceleration, the fly line will slide toward you and sag, and you'll create slack between your rod tip and the water.

Keep in mind that the fly-casting stroke is a continuous acceleration. Although you must begin to lift the fly line slowly from the water, you must lift it continually faster throughout the stroke. If you don't, the rod will not load, and you'll have no hope of getting the fly line to straighten behind you on the back cast. The "trick" to lifting a fly line off the water is to lift slowly enough that you do not rip the line, but increasingly fast enough so that the line does not have time to slide toward you and sag. You can only develop this over time with practice.

Once you begin to lift the fly line from the water during the loading move, you must commit to the stroke, and you must continue to accelerate throughout. That is, you cannot hesitate. If you hesitate at any point in the lift, however briefly, any load that you've put on the rod will dissipate, and the cast will be compromised. Also, there can be no hesitation between the loading move and the power snap. Although we can describe the cast as having two stages of acceleration, these stages must flow together seamlessly: *the rod must move through the casting arc in one fluid motion.* Although you may get away with a brief hesitation when lifting a short line, you'll never get away with this when you're lifting a long line from the water.

The tendency of many would-be fly-fishers who have spin-fishing experience is to simply wind up and put all of their effort into the forward stroke—as they would do with a spinning rod. They're not used to having to cast backward. Keep in mind that in terms of fly-rod mechanics, the forward cast and back cast are identical casts delivered in opposite directions. You need to use as much force on your back cast as you do on your forward cast. On your back-cast stroke, you must start slowly, accelerate continuously, and stop abruptly. To execute a proper forward cast, you must first get the fly line straight behind you.

Some fly-fishers try to lift the line off the water using wrist movement alone. If you do this, you're sure to move the rod tip through a curved path. Keep in mind that the loop of line will assume any shape that the path of the rod tip has traveled. If you lift line from the water by opening your wrist, you'll rip your loop open. Keep in mind that the fly-casting stroke is a full-arm movement that uses your upper arm and forearm as well as your wrist. Your back cast should begin with your wrist in the bent-forward position, with the butt of the rod parallel with the underside of your forearm, and it should stay in this position until the end of the loading move (see photo 3). The wrist doesn't come into play until the second part of the stroke: the power-snap portion of the cast.

A number of fly-fishers have a tendency to begin their back-cast strokes with their wrists not fully in the bent-forward position. That is, the back cast begins with the butt of the rod less than parallel with the underside of the forearm. The problem with this is that if you begin the back cast with your wrist not fully bent forward, you're much more likely to open it beyond the straight position during the stroke, opening your loop wide. Each time you prepare to make your pick-up-and-lay-down cast, make sure the rod butt is parallel with the underside of your forearm. This is one of a number of fine points that you should check each and every time you prepare to make any cast until it becomes as natural to you as breathing.

All this might seem like slavish attention to detail, but it is such attention that enables a handful of fly casters to rise above the rest. An effortless fly cast is beautiful to watch, yet the efforts that go into building that cast are fairly tedious. When you watch a masterful caster unroll a fly line to the opposite bank with about as much difficulty as you would have licking an ice-cream cone, understand that you're witnessing the fruits of devoted practice and effort. Countless hours spent on fishless ponds and grassy fields, checking the position of the wrist at the beginning of the stroke, the direction the thumb is pointed at the conclusion of the stroke, studying the shape of the loop when you stop the rod here . . . and here . . . and here—the myriad details that the vast majority of fly-fishers dismiss as trivial.

Occasionally I'll see a fly-fisher who has developed the bad habit of twisting her wrist to turn her rod hand outward during the back-cast stroke. Although this habit is much more prevalent among fly-fishers casting from the open stance, keep in mind that whatever your rod hand does during the stroke is going to be reflected in, and magnified at, the rod tip. Lefty Kreh has stated that the thumb of your rod hand functions as a sort of "rudder" for your cast. That's an excel-lent analogy. If your rod hand turns outward during the casting stroke—that is, if you turn the rudder during the stroke—you'll put a decided hook into your cast.

Before we discuss the problems inherent in the back cast's second stage of acceleration, I'd like to say a few words about the efficiency of your rod-arm mechanics.

Many fly-fishers tend to cast with their rod hand significantly out-side their shoulder—actually, I've seen many more fly-fishers cast this way than not (including a number of fly-fishers of note). Although you may be able to cast sufficiently to catch fish this way, it's a less efficient set of mechanics than the one I've detailed here. The farther your rod hand gets from your body, the less strength you have. To cast with your rod hand significantly outside your body is the equivalent of trying to do pushups with your hands outstretched to your sides, or trying to curl a dumbbell held at nearly arm's length. Casting with your rod hand held well outside your body will fatigue you much more quickly, particularly with heavier fly tackle. Also, this set of me-chanics uses shoulder muscles to do the primary work of the casting stroke (rather than the biceps and triceps)—a critical consideration for anyone who has a shoulder condition, or anyone hoping to avoid one. With your rod hand held far away from your body, there's a much greater chance that it will move your hand through a curved path, opening your loops wide. Finally, keep in mind that the greater the distance between your rod hand and your eye, the less accurate your casts will tend to be.

Casting with your rod hand outside your shoulder *(above)* requires more strength, and is less accurate, than keeping your forearm and upper arm in alignment *(below)*.

Casting vertically from a closed stance requires you to keep your forearm and upper arm aligned throughout the casting sequence. This is extremely efficient because it makes full use of your natural strength, allocating the primary work on the back cast to the biceps and the primary work on the forward cast to the triceps. Your under-standing of efficiency and your ability to make efficient casts are pre-requisite to your becoming a good distance caster.

This set of mechanics may strike you as narrow or rigid—as if you're being forced to cast inside a box. However, I assure you this is the best, fastest way to learn the fundamentals. Casting vertically from a closed stance minimizes the number of mistakes it's possible to make and goes a long way toward forcing good fly-casting form upon the student. And that is not such a bad thing.

The **vertical plane** is the most accurate plane in which to cast, as this is the plane in which your rod hand is closest to your eye. Al-though you may be fairly accurate casting off-vertical or even sidearm (which we explore in lessons 5 and 7), you'll never be as accurate, consistently, as you will in the vertical plane (though in actual fish-ing situations you certainly will have to be able to cast in all planes).

We now come to the second stage of the acceleration, the power-

snap portion of the back-cast stroke. I don't particularly like the terms *power snap*, *power stroke*, or *speed-up-and-stop* to denote the second part of the acceleration. More precisely, I don't like the words *power* or *speed* associated with this part of the stroke. It's not that I feel I can come up with a better term; frankly, I don't think any two- or several-word term can accurately describe the action. The problem I have with attaching the words *power* or *speed* to that part of the stroke is that the tendency of many fly-fishers, both beginners as well as experienced anglers, is to use a lot of power, a lot of speed, to yank the fly out of the water.

Remember that the leader and fly weigh almost nothing—you literally could lift them with the muscles in a single eyelid—and they have virtually no surface tension. Once you lift the fly line to the line-leader connection on the loading move, you've broken all the surface tension of the fly line; at this point, it's extremely easy to pick the leader and fly out of the water.

If you've loaded the rod properly during the loading move, you've already done nine-tenths the work. Keep in mind that it's the spring-flex action of the rod, and not the movement of your rod arm, that propels the back cast.

It's also important to bear in mind that the "power snap" has only two functions: the first function is to complete the loading of the rod; the second function is to stop the rod abruptly to unload it. When you begin the power-snap portion of the cast, the rod is already loaded significantly (see photo 3). When your wrist moves from the bent-forward position, through the 45-degree arc to reach the straight position, the loading of the rod is complete, and the rod has stopped abruptly to unload. Your rod arm does not need to move another fraction of an inch.

When I'm holding the rod handle with the key grip, my index finger is directly opposite my thumb on the cork. During the second part of the back-cast stroke I pull back slightly on the cork with my index finger as my wrist snaps from bent-forward to straight. I actually have the sensation that I'm picking the fly out of the water with my index finger. It's that subtle, and it's that effortless. Picking the fly out of the water doesn't require any force. To yank the fly out of the water with power is not only unnecessary, it will destroy your back cast.

Some anglers open their wrists on the power snap so that the rod butt is at a 90-degree angle to their forearm, or nearly so. This is often—but not always—related to using too much force during the second stage of acceleration. If you break your wrist on the back cast, you're going to dump your cast into the ground or water behind you.

On the back-cast power snap, your rod butt should come out from the underside of your forearm at no more than a 45-degree angle. This ensures that your loop will remain tight, and that your cast will unroll upward rather than downward.

Breaking your wrist on the back cast will cause you to dump your cast into the ground or water behind you. Keep in mind that wherever the line coming off your thumbnail is pointed when you stop the rod on the back cast, that's where the cast will unroll.

Always keep in mind that your thumb functions as an aiming device in fly casting—on the back cast as well as the forward cast. Imagine a line going through your thumb almost perpendicular to it. Wherever this line is pointed when you stop the rod, that's where your cast is going to go.

If you break your wrist on the back cast, the line coming off your thumbnail will be pointed down at the ground or water behind you—and that's exactly where your cast will unroll. On a good pick-up-and-lay-down cast, your rod hand stops on the back-cast stroke so that the line coming off your thumbnail is pointed up at an angle behind you—and that's where your cast will unroll as well.

Rather than thinking of "opening" your wrist during the power-snap portion of the back cast, it may help you to think of simply "cracking" your wrist as you squeeze the rod to stop it dead. This mental distinction helped me to gain command of my own stroke, and if you're repeatedly breaking your wrist on the back cast, it may help you as well.

A good back-cast stroke concludes with the line coming off your thumbnail pointed up at an angle behind you.

Your ability to feel the fly line straighten behind you on the back cast is critical to your timing of the forward stroke. The rod will not begin to load on the forward stroke until the fly line is in a straight line behind you. If you begin your forward stroke before the back cast has finished unrolling, you'll steal some power from the forward cast. If your line is not laying out completely on the delivery, but landing in a pile, this could very well be the problem. If you begin the forward stroke well before the back cast has straightened, you'll kill the forward cast completely.

If you're having trouble feeling the fly line straighten on the back cast, try accentuating the stop at the end of the back-cast stroke. That is, focus on stopping the rod dead in its tracks. Remember that the more abruptly you stop the rod, the more power there'll be in the cast. If your back cast unrolls with a little more power, you're more likely to feel the line straighten.

You need to begin the forward stroke the instant the back cast straightens. When the back cast straightens, the fly line will be taut, as if someone were pulling it from behind you to stretch it. If you wait a fraction of a second longer, the line will lose its tautness and begin to fall. Although you may still be able to deliver the cast, it will not be nearly as efficient. And if you wait too long between the time the fly line straightens and the time you begin the forward stroke, the fly will hit the ground or water behind you. A good fly caster begins her forward stroke while the fly line is still taut. This requires precise timing, and you may not get it right the first time you cast—nor the first hundred times—but this is the precision to which you must aspire.

The tendency of many beginners, and too many experienced fly-fishers, is to lock their upper arms in place during the pick-up-and-lay-down cast and execute the cast using only their forearm and wrist.

1. A straight-line path of your rod hand produces a tight loop.
2. A curved path of your rod hand produces a wide loop or nonloop.

You'll probably get away with this with a very short line, but never with a line of even moderate length. Again, during the casting stroke, your rod hand must travel along a straight-line path, both on the back cast and the forward cast. The only way to accommodate that straight line is to use a full-arm movement: upper arm, forearm, and wrist. Imagine standing sideways to a chalkboard, the chalkboard next to your shoulder. Imagine also that you have a piece of chalk under your thumb, lying perpendicular to your thumb, and one end of the piece of chalk is touching the board. If you were asked to draw a straight line on the board that slopes downward at about 45 degrees—this roughly would be the path of your forward stroke—the only way you could accomplish this would be with a full-arm movement. If you were to attempt to draw this line by locking your upper arm in place, you would be able to draw only a curved line. On a good pick-up-and-lay-down cast, the elbow raises on the back-cast stroke to lift the line off the water, and then lowers again on the forward stroke. This full-arm movement is the only way to maintain a straight-line path of the rod hand, and hence a straight-line path of the rod tip. Remember that your cast will assume any shape that the path of your rod hand (and rod tip) has traveled. A straight-line path of your rod hand produces a tight loop; a curved path produces a wide loop or nonloop.

Once again, it's critical for you to remember that the thumb of your rod hand functions as an aiming device, on the forward cast as well as the back cast. On a good forward stroke, your thumb moves

The clock-face analogy may help you tighten your loop and aim your cast. Determine where on the clock face the shaft of the rod is stopping when you form an open loop, and then try to stop the rod higher.

along the hand-target line and stops along this line. This produces a tight loop and aims your cast wherever the line coming off the pad of your thumb is pointed. If, however, your thumb veers off this straight-line path, you'll rip your loop open. If you end the forward stroke with the line coming off the pad of your thumb pointed down at the water at your feet, that's where your cast will go.

If you're having trouble forming a tight loop on your forward cast, it may help you to imagine that you're standing against a clock face. Twelve o'clock is directly overhead, and 9 o'clock is directly in front of you. Determine where on the clock face the shaft of your rod is pointed when you stop the rod to form an open loop, and then simply stop it higher on the clock face. That is, if the shaft of the rod is stopping at 9:30 for your poor loop, stop it instead at 10 o'clock. This clock-face analogy is simply another convention, another way to think about the cast, and is far from being a fly-casting cure-all. However, it may help you to understand the relationship between your rod hand and your target, and in particular, the role of your thumb as an aiming device.

Some fly-fishers destroy their forward cast by running the cast and follow-through together, ripping their loop open. Remember that the forward stroke and follow-through are two separate parts of the cast. Follow-through is outside the casting stroke itself and is done without force. You must first stop the rod on the forward stroke and allow the loop to form. After the loop has formed, and the line has begun unrolling toward your target, then you can follow through with the rod tip down to the water. If you're having trouble with this, you could try making the cast without following through to the water. That is, keep the rod positioned where you stop it at the end of the forward stroke and let the cast unroll completely. When you're fishing, you'll have to use follow-through (to keep the slack out of the fly line and to put yourself in good position to make another back cast), but at this stage, omitting follow-through may help you learn to form a good loop.

A great many casters use too much speed or power on the delivery. If your fly line straightens on the forward cast, and then bounces back at you and lands on the water with a lot of slack, you're using too much force on your forward stroke.

As I've said, I don't particularly like to associate the words *speed* or *power* with the second part of the stroke, for these terms seem to imply that the purpose of the second part of the stroke is to impart a forward "thrust" to your cast. This, I believe, is one of the most prevalent misconceptions in fly casting. The pushing-pulling motion you execute with your rod hand during the second stage of the stroke (*power snap, power stroke, speed-up-and-stop,* or whatever you want to call it) has only two functions, and they bear repeating: the first function is to complete the loading of the rod; the second function is to stop the rod abruptly to unload it. Stopping the rod abruptly triggers the rod's spring-flex action to fire the fly line forward. It's the positive stop of the rod, and *not* how quickly you move the rod through the stroke or how much force you use, that makes the line unroll. For any given cast, use only as much force as you need to get the line and leader to turn over crisply and land on the water delicately. Keep in mind the analogy of an automobile hitting a brick wall at 50 mph: the automobile will stop abruptly, but so would one traveling only 5 mph. To deliver a fly only 30 feet, the so-called power snap is relatively soft. For a very short cast, as I might use when fishing a small stream,

A tailing loop forms when the rod unloads such that the rod tip is above, rather than below, the path of the following fly line. The legs of the loop are crossed rather than open-ended. For a short cast, a tailing loop is most often caused by a very short, jerky casting stroke.

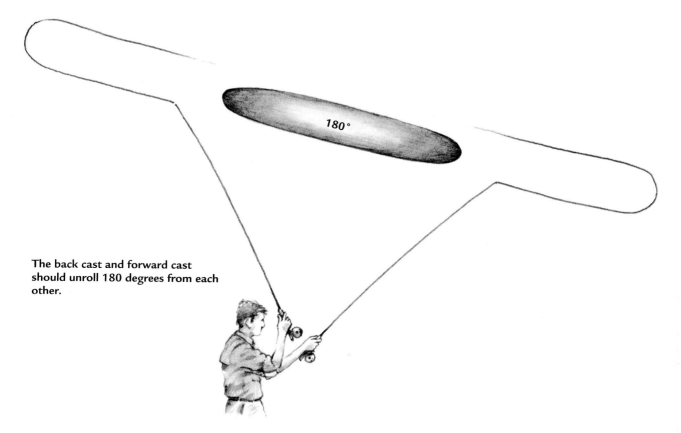

The back cast and forward cast should unroll 180 degrees from each other.

it's as if my wrist simply "clicks" into the bent-forward position.

Virtually all fly-fishers have trouble, from time to time, with knots tied in their leaders. We call these **wind knots** (see page 14), although they have nothing to do with wind. These so-called wind knots are caused by **tailing loops**.

Many casters have a tendency to unroll their cast high above the target. If you unroll your cast 6 feet above the target, the slightest breeze can sweep the fly off course as it settles. On the pick-up-and-lay-down cast, unroll your cast very close to the target. Unrolling your leader just above the target allows you to be more accurate.

On the pick-up-and-lay-down cast, the back cast and forward cast unroll 180 degrees from each other. The shorter the line, the steeper the cast. A very short line produces a very high back cast (see top left photo next page). For a longer line, the angle will be less steep (see top right photo). For your longest pick-up-and-lay-down cast, the back cast will unroll only slightly above **the horizontal**—the horizontal being an imaginary line that comes off your rod tip and runs parallel with the ground or water (see bottom photo).

The longer the line you must lift from the water, the longer your back-cast stroke must be. To lift a very short line from the water, you need only a very short back-cast stroke. For a longer line, you'll need

The shorter the line, the steeper the cast. A very short line produces a very high back cast.

For a longer line, the angle will be less steep.

On your longest pick-up-and-lay-down cast, the back cast will unroll only slightly above the horizontal.

a longer back-cast stroke. For your longest back-cast stroke—with as much as 40 feet of fly line outside the rod tip, depending on your height—your stroke will end with your forearm crashing into your biceps. This is a literal crash. When your forearm hits your biceps, your rod hand is going to stop abruptly, and this positive stop is going to transfer all the power from the loaded rod into your back cast. This is called a **body block**, and I want you to pay a lot of attention to this, because this concept is critical to your becoming a good distance caster. Remember that the more abruptly you can stop the rod, the more power you can put into the cast. Utilizing this body block allows you to make a long, powerful back cast with very little effort. If you didn't use this body block, you'd have to use strength to stop the rod. And which would stop a moving car more abruptly: applying brakes or hitting a brick wall? The body block gives your rod hand a wall to hit. Remember, however, that you'll use the body block only on your longest back-cast stroke.

Lawn Casting

The main problem with learning to cast vertically from the closed stance is that you cannot watch your back cast. Casting horizontally on the lawn will allow you to see your entire cast, its individual parts, and how they work. It will also allow you to see your mistakes and help you figure out how to correct them. *This exercise is the single most beneficial practice routine that any fly-fisher can perform.*

Begin by laying your rod on the ground with about 12 feet of fly line outside the rod tip. Next, lay out the fly line 90 degrees off each side of the rod tip and place a target at each end. I like to use plastic bread baskets, but you can use books, stones, or whatever. Line up with your shoulders square to the line of the targets, and with the face of your reel and the palm of your rod hand facing upward. The object of this exercise is to use a horizontal casting stroke to lay both the back cast and forward cast out directly in line with the targets in a tight loop. (See art next page.)

Make a cast, let the loop fall to the ground completely, and analyze it. You can see that if you move your hand in a curved path on your

For your longest back-cast stroke (about 40 feet of fly line outside the rod tip, depending on your height), your stroke will end with your forearm crashing into your biceps. This literal crash is the body block for the back-cast stroke.

To begin the horizontal lawn casting exercise, lay your rod on the ground with about 12 feet of fly line outside the rod tip. Then lay out the fly line 90 degrees off each side of the rod tip and place a target at each end.

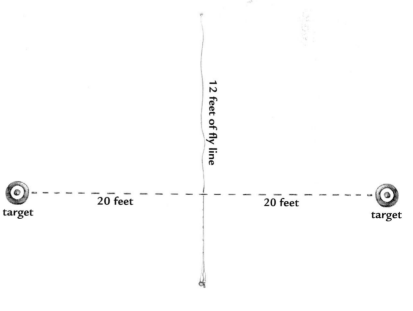

12 feet of fly line

target — 20 feet — 20 feet — target

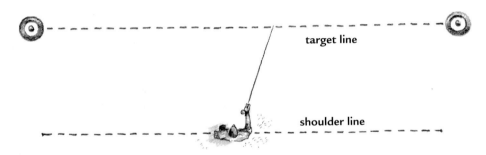

target line

shoulder line

Line up with your shoulders square to the line of the targets, and with the face of your reel and the palm of your rod hand facing upwards.

Use a horizontal casting stroke to lay both the back cast and forward cast out directly in line with the targets in a tight loop.

forward stroke (as you might do if you run the cast together with follow-through), you'll get a wide loop. And if you break your wrist on your back cast, you'll widen the loop also. To form a tight loop and make the line lay out straight in line with the targets, you need to move your rod hand in a straight line, parallel with the line of the targets.

Casting horizontally on the lawn, you'll clearly see that the path of your rod hand determines the path of your rod tip. Remember that a straight-line path of the rod tip forms a tight loop. Watch the rod tip as it moves through the casting arc. It must follow along the straight line that exists between your two targets.

Many fly-fishers have trouble when first attempting this exercise because they allow their elbows to escape their sides during the stroke. Holding your elbow away from your side during the stroke en-

sures that you will move your rod hand, and hence the rod tip, in a curved path, producing a wide loop (see photo next page).

You can unroll a very short line with virtually no loading move, using just the power snap (see art next page). A longer line is going to require a loading move; that is, you're going to have to get everything moving before you form the loop and make the cast. With a longer line you'll have to follow through a bit after you stop the rod at the end of each power snap to give yourself room to make a loading move (see art page 63). Follow-through is a continuation of the straight-line path begun by the casting stroke. Follow-through after the back cast is called **drift**. (Notice that drift and follow-through occupy the same space within the casting stroke or arc as does the loading move.) We'll learn more about drift in lesson 6.

To get the line to unroll crisply, you must start slowly, accelerate gradually, and stop abruptly, on both the back cast *and* the forward cast. The casting stroke must be smooth. A jerky stroke will destroy the cast.

This exercise is not about making lots of casts. Rather, it's about learning something from every cast you make. Watch your loop of line on each cast. *Your loop of line is your single best piece of data for self-analysis, for your loop of line tells you exactly what your rod hand and*

1. If you move your hand in a curved path on your forward stroke, you'll get a wide loop. **2.** If you break your wrist on your back cast, you'll widen the loop also. **3.** To form a tight loop, you need to move your rod hand in a straight line, parallel with the line of the targets.

Holding your elbow away from your side during the stroke ensures that you will move your rod hand, and hence the rod tip, in a curved path, producing a wide loop.

rod tip did during the casting stroke. Let each cast fall to the ground and take the time to analyze what happened. Each cast has something to teach you.

This exercise is deceptive in its simplicity—so much so that most fly-casting students forget about it immediately after learning it, and they never work with it again. I can't emphasize enough that *this ex-*

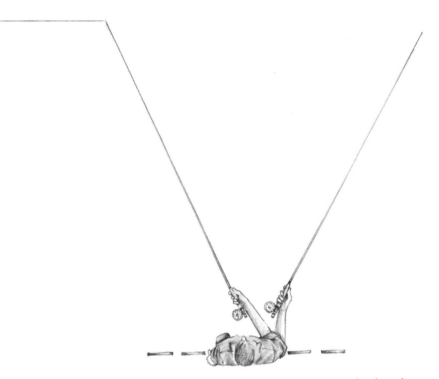

A very short line you can cast with virtually no loading move, using just the power snap.

A longer line requires a loading move to get everything in motion before you make the cast. With a longer line you'll have to follow through after each power snap to give yourself room to make a loading move on the next stroke. Follow-through after the back-cast stroke is called *drift.*

ercise is the single best tool you have for building a solid basic stroke. This horizontal lawn casting exercise is your actual fly cast, only laid on its side and frozen in time. Ironing out your problems horizontally on the lawn will help you immeasurably when you bring the cast back up to the vertical plane. Learn this simple exercise and you'll have gone a long way toward mastering your cast.

False Casting

In lesson 2 we explored the pick-up-and-lay-down cast, which consists of only two strokes: a single back cast followed by a single forward cast. When you're actually fishing, however, you won't always pick the fly off the water and put it back down immediately—sometimes you'll keep it airborne for several strokes before delivering it. This is called **false casting**.

In fly-fishing false casting has several functions, the most common of which is to shake the water off a dry fly so that it will float again. You can also use false casting to change direction, gradually rotating your upper body toward your target as you hold the line aloft for several strokes. On moving water, this is usually to deliver a fly upstream of where the current carried your fly.

When you learn to use your line hand (see pages 70–74), you can use false casting to judge distance. That is, you'll watch where your leader and fly unroll in relation to your target. You'll then lengthen, or shorten, the fly line as needed so that the leader and fly unroll directly above your target.

You'll learn to false cast first using only your rod hand (as you did for both previous lessons), trapping the fly line under your middle finger to control it.

Begin with 12 feet of fly line outside the rod tip. The fly line should be lying straight out in front of you on the water with all the slack removed, and your rod tip should be touching the water. Lift the line from the water in a loading move, exactly as if you were making a pick-up-and-lay-down cast (photo 1, next page). After you've completed the back cast and the line has unrolled behind you almost completely, begin your forward stroke (photo 2). After you stop the rod on the forward stroke and the rod unloads, the loop will begin to unroll toward the target (photo 3); just before the line has unrolled completely (the end of the fly line will be shaped like a candy cane), begin another back-cast stroke (photo 4).

1. To execute a false-casting sequence, lift the line from the water as if you were beginning a pick-up-and-lay-down cast. 2. When your back cast has unrolled almost completely, begin your forward stroke. 3 and 4. Just before the forward cast has straightened (the end of the fly line will be shaped like a candy cane), begin another back-cast stroke.

False Casting #1

False Casting #2

False Casting #3

False Casting #4

Unlike the pick-up-and-lay-down cast, in which you begin the forward stroke just as the back cast has straightened behind you, when false casting it's important to begin each stroke *just before* the previous cast has unrolled completely. This allows you to bring the fly line, leader, and fly through a smooth change of direction. If you wait until the fly line has straightened completely before beginning each stroke, your false-casting sequence will have a clunky feel and appearance. Also, as we learned in lesson 2, as soon as the cast unrolls completely, the fly line will begin to fall. If, during your false-casting sequence, you allow the fly line to begin to fall, there's a good chance your fly will hit the ground or tick the water (particularly if you are false casting a longer length of line).

As we also learned in lesson 2, you don't want to begin the casting stroke *too* soon. If you begin the stroke before enough fly line has had a chance to unroll, you won't be able to load the rod, and the cast will collapse (see photos 6 and 7, next page).

When false casting from a closed stance, you won't be able to watch your back cast unroll; however, you will be able to watch your forward cast. The amount of time it takes for your forward cast to unroll will give you a good sense of how long it should take for your back cast to unroll, too, as well as a good sense of the cadence of the false-casting sequence. False casting horizontally above the lawn will give you an even better sense of the timing required.

Despite whatever opportunity you may have to watch part, or all, of your cast, perfect timing cannot be accomplished either visually or mentally. In fly casting, perfect timing depends on *feeling*. As your casting stroke develops, you'll be able to feel the weight of the fly line against the rod tip; this weight will increase gradually as the cast unrolls. You'll feel this through the fingers of your rod hand, which is your only connection to the fly rod. This feeling will always be fairly subtle, but it will become more noticeable as your skills progress. Developing this feeling will give you a sense of being constantly connected with the weight of the fly line throughout each cast. This

As soon as the cast unrolls completely, the fly line will begin to fall. If you allow it to fall, there's a good chance your fly will hit the ground or tick the water.

False Casting #5

False Casting #6

False Casting #7

If you begin the casting stroke before the majority of the fly line has un- rolled, you won't be able to load the rod, and the sequence will collapse.

For accuracy you'll unroll your fly close to the water, just above your target. Your rod hand will move up- ward and backward on the back-cast stroke and forward and downward on the forward-cast stroke.

phenomenon adds a tactile aspect to your awareness of the unrolling cast. With practice, you'll be able to distinguish, and act upon, the difference between a cast that's almost unrolled completely and one that's fully extended—a difference in timing that amounts to a frac- tion of a second.

For accuracy you'll unroll your fly close to the water, just above your target. Your rod hand will move upward and backward on the back-cast stroke and forward and downward on the forward-cast stroke—but again, always along a straight-line path. You can hold the fly line aloft for as many strokes as you wish. When it looks as if your fly line is unrolling directly above your target, present the

False Casting #8

False Casting #9

fly by simply following through to the water with your rod tip.

When false casting to change direction, it's OK if your cast unrolls farther above the water. Your rod hand will still move in a straight line—but this time the path is less steep. However, your delivery will be most accurate if the leader unrolls just above the target.

False casting with only 12 feet of fly line outside the rod tip requires very little power. Whatever length of line you're casting, use only enough force to get the line and leader to turn over crisply. Use too much power and you'll shock the cast.

When you feel comfortable false casting with 12 feet of fly line outside the rod tip, increase the length to 15 feet. With 15 feet of fly line outside the rod tip, you'll have to use a slightly longer casting stroke to get the fly line to turn over. Your timing will change slightly; you'll have to wait a bit longer for this line to unroll.

When you're comfortable with 15 feet of line, lengthen it to 20. Again, your timing changes. You have to wait longer still between casts. Your casting stroke lengthens slightly, and perhaps you need to use a bit more force to keep the fly line airborne. However, use only enough force to turn everything over crisply. Always bear in mind that fly casting should be beautiful to watch.

With practice (and after you learn drift and follow-through, which we'll discuss in lesson 6), you may be able to false cast with 30 or more

When false casting to change direction, your cast may unroll farther above the water.

With practice, you may be able to false cast with 30 or more feet of fly line outside the rod tip, which will allow you to present a fly nearly 50 feet.

False Casting #10

feet of fly line outside the rod tip. Assuming you're using a 9-foot rod and a 9-foot leader, 30 feet of fly line outside the rod tip will allow you to present a fly nearly 50 feet. With a 50-foot cast, you'll be prepared to fish for any gamefish species in the world, in freshwater or salt.

When first learning to false cast, you may wish to hold the line in the air for ten strokes or more before you present the yarn fly to the target. This is fine, as it will help you to develop the necessary rhythm. When you're actually fishing, however, there will be no need for such a drawn-out casting sequence. Many beginners, as well as too many experienced fly-fishers, false cast excessively. Under most circumstances, even the most water-logged fly should need no more than three back casts (a total of six strokes) to make it float again. The same number of strokes should allow you to pick your fly out of the water directly downstream and present it directly across. A large part of becoming a good fly caster is becoming an efficient fly caster. When you're fishing, use only as many false casts as you need. It may sound like a cliché to say that you won't catch a fish with your fly in the air—but it's also true.

The Line Hand

Until now you've cast with the fly line trapped under the middle finger of your rod hand. This anchors the fly line to the rod and allows you to develop your rod-arm mechanics independent of the line hand. When actually fishing, however, you'll seldom cast with the line trapped in your rod hand. Therefore, we must now address the functions of the line hand.

One function of the line hand is to strip line from the reel.

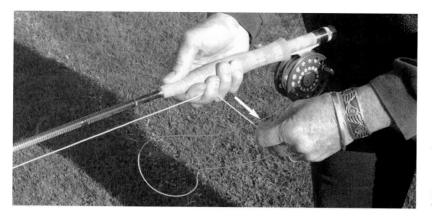

You'll retrieve fly line by hooking the line under the middle finger of your rod hand to control it, and then stripping in line from behind the middle finger.

The line hand has several functions in fly-fishing and fly casting. Perhaps the most obvious function is to strip line from the reel. You'll also use your line hand to retrieve line: hooking line under the middle finger of your rod hand to control it, and then stripping in line from behind the middle finger.

As far as casting is concerned, the primary function of the line hand is to maintain tension on the fly line throughout the entire casting stroke. If you fail to do this—that is, you introduce slack into the cast—you'll steal some of the power from the cast, and you'll likely compromise its accuracy. Although you may never notice the negative effects an inch or two of slack can create in a short cast, you will notice them on a long cast. To make a long cast you must get the full potential out of the rod. A well-trained line hand assures that you cast efficiently.

To make a pick-up-and-lay-down cast using your line hand properly, begin with 25 feet of fly line stripped off the reel. Stroke line across the water until all of it is outside the rod tip and lying in a pile on the water (see photo on page 28). This should give you a little more than 15 feet of line outside the rod tip. Trap the line under the middle finger of your rod hand and roll cast it so that it's lying straight in front of you. Strip in enough fly line so that you have only 12 feet, plus the leader, outside the rod tip.

Keeping the rod tip close to the water with no slack, grasp the fly line between the thumb and index finger of your line hand and release the line from your rod hand. Move your line hand about 2 feet out from the shaft of the rod. You've now formed a sort of triangle with the rod shaft, the fly line, and an imaginary line running between your two hands (see photo next page). This triangle should be wide enough that you could, if you wanted to, fit your head through it.

To maintain tension on the fly line throughout the casting sequence, you'll need to move both hands in unison on both strokes. During the back cast, your line hand will raise the same amount as does the rod hand; on the forward cast, it will move forward in uni-

Grasp the fly line between the thumb and index finger of your line hand and release the line from your rod hand. Move your line hand about 2 feet out from the shaft of the rod. You've now formed a sort of triangle with the rod shaft, the fly line, and an imaginary line running between your two hands.

During the entire casting sequence, both hands move in unison.

son with the rod hand as well; and while the loop of line is unrolling toward the target, both hands will follow through. In fact, your rod hand and line hand mirror each other so closely during the casting sequence, it's as if you are holding a rod in each of them. Moving your hands in unison during both strokes as well as during follow-through keeps a constant length of line between the line hand and the first stripping guide, maintaining line tension throughout the entire casting sequence.

If you were to keep your line hand stationary during the casting sequence, your rod hand would move toward your line hand on the forward stroke; you would, in effect, feed slack into your forward cast, stealing power from the cast and compromising its accuracy. To maintain line tension you must maintain an equal distance between your rod hand and line hand during the forward casting stroke.

During the casting sequence it's OK if your line hand is slightly lower than your rod hand—you may even be more comfortable this way—as long as both hands move in unison, and an equal distance to each other, during the casting sequence.

Learn to use your line hand first using the pick-up-and-lay-down cast. When you get comfortable with this, begin to use it for false casting; for this is how you'll cast when you're actually fishing. In lesson 4 we'll discuss the additional functions the line hand performs in fly casting.

I've just explained how to move your hands in unison during the casting sequence in order to maintain line tension, and I'm convinced this is the best, fastest way to learn how to do so. However, I must admit that, for the most part, this is not how I do it myself. As you progress as a fly caster, and your awareness of line tension becomes second nature, you probably will be much more comfortable keeping your line hand around waist level. During the back-cast

If you were to keep your line hand stationary during the casting sequence, you would feed slack into your forward cast, stealing power from the cast and compromising its accuracy.

Holding your line hand at waist level is the best way to learn to use it while roll casting.

stroke, your rod hand actually moves away from your line hand. During the forward stroke, the line hand moves backward and downward slightly to maintain tension. As the forward cast is unrolling, the line hand raises slightly to position itself for the next cast; the fly line is kept taut through the force of the unrolling forward cast (see lesson 5). Holding your line hand at waist level is the best way to learn to use it while roll casting (see photos previous page). To execute such a sequence requires a good peripheral awareness of the interaction between rod and line, which you'll develop over time with practice.

Shooting Line

Shooting line is a way to increase the length of your cast to a distance greater than the amount of line you've held in the air. After the rod has unloaded on your final forward stroke and the loop of line has begun to unroll toward the target, you'll release the line trapped in your line hand. The force of the unrolling cast will take several additional feet (or a number of yards) of line along with it, extending the length of your delivery. (As a rule of thumb, I'll shoot line when I have to reach a target that is more than 40 feet away.)

To shoot line for the first time, begin with a total of 15 feet of fly line, plus your leader, outside the rod tip. That is, when the line and leader are fully extended in front of you, the yarn fly will be a total of 33 feet away from you (assuming you are using a 9-foot rod and a 9-foot leader). The line should be lying on the water in front of you with all the slack removed.

Strip in 3 feet of line for a total of 12 feet outside the rod tip.

Pick the fly line off the water and false cast it, moving your rod hand and line hand in unison.

Shooting Line #1

Pick the fly line off the water and false cast it, moving your rod hand and line hand in unison.

False cast several times to gain command of the cast and get a feel for the timing of holding the 12 feet of fly line airborne. Plan on making a delivery.

When shooting line on your delivery, your timing changes on your final back cast. Rather than beginning your final back cast just *before* your line has unrolled completely, as you would for all of your other false casts, let your final back cast straighten completely (as you would for the back cast of a pick-up-and-lay-down cast). You'll feel this as a tug on the rod tip. The force of the back cast straightening behind you will pull your rod tip into a slight bend. That is, when the fly line straightens behind you, your rod will be **preloaded**.

Make your forward cast. After you've stopped the rod on the forward cast and the loop of line has formed, simply release the fly line in your line hand. If you've done everything correctly, the force of the unrolling cast will take the additional 3 feet of fly line with it. As with every cast, as the loop of line unrolls toward your target, you'll follow through with the rod tip to the water.

The timing of the forward stroke is critical to your getting the

The force of your back cast straightening will pull the rod into a slight bend. That is, your rod will be preloaded for the forward stroke.

Shooting Line #2

Shooting Line #3

After you've stopped the rod on the forward cast and the loop of line has formed, release the fly line in your line hand. The force of the unrolling cast will take the additional 3 feet of fly line with it.

most out of the cast with the least amount of effort. You must begin the forward stroke the instant the back cast has straightened—and not a fraction of a second later. You'll feel a subtle tug on the rod tip as your back cast straightens, and for an instant you'll experience the feeling of the airborne fly line stretched taut against the rod tip, flexing it backward slightly. *You must begin the forward stroke at this instant.* If you wait even a fraction of a second after you feel the tug, the preload will vanish and your line will lose its tautness and begin to fall. You may still be able to shoot line and deliver the fly, but such a cast is not nearly as efficient as it could be.

As a beginner, you probably won't be able to time your casts perfectly. However, as you become, through practice, more cognizant of the fly line's weight against the rod tip, and you can utilize this feeling to help you execute your stroke, your casts will become increasingly efficient.

The most common mistake for casters learning to shoot line is to release the line too soon. If you release the line during any part of the casting stroke, you'll kill the cast. You must complete the forward stroke—the rod must be stopped, and the loop must already be formed—before you release the line.

Use the loop of line as your visual cue. Once you've stopped the rod on the forward stroke and you see the loop of line ahead of the rod tip, simply open the fingers of your line hand (or stick out the middle finger of your rod hand, for a single-handed shoot) and release the line completely.

Another common mistake is to overpower the delivery such that you rip your loop open and kill the cast. Very often I'll see fly-fishers make three or four perfect false casts, and then they'll slam the delivery, rip their loop open, and destroy their cast.

If your form and timing are good on your delivery stroke, you'll easily be able to shoot the additional 3 feet of fly line. You don't

Shooting Line #4

If you release the line during any part of the casting stroke, you'll kill the cast.

The Single-Handed Shoot

If you have trouble shooting line using both hands, it may help to try it first using only your rod hand. Trap the line under the middle finger of your rod hand with the 3 additional feet of line hanging from the reel, then false cast several times to gain command of the stroke. After you stop the rod on your final forward cast, and you see that the loop has formed and begun to unroll toward the target, stick your middle finger straight out to release the line completely.

To shoot line with your rod hand alone, trap the fly line under the middle finger of your rod hand with 3 additional feet of line hanging from the reel. False cast several times to gain command of the stroke.

After you stop the rod on your final forward cast, stick your middle finger straight out to release the line completely.

need to add any additional power. At this short distance, your delivery cast should look no different from any of your false casts.

Work with a total of 15 feet of fly line until you're comfortable with it, and then lengthen it to 20 feet. Hold 15 feet of line outside the rod tip as you false cast, and then shoot the additional 5 feet on the delivery.

The more of the fly line's weight you have outside the rod tip, the easier it's going to be to shoot line, and the more line you'll be able to shoot. If you can hold 20 feet of fly line in the air as you false cast and shoot an additional 5 feet on the delivery, assuming that you have a 9-foot rod and a 9-foot leader, you can deliver a fly in excess of 40 feet. That's more than far enough to fly fish for any species of freshwater fish on just about any body of water.

As your line-hand skills develop, you'll be able to shoot a bit of line after each forward false cast, to lengthen the amount of line you have outside the rod tip. To do this, you'll release the line briefly after the rod unloads, allowing a few inches of line to shoot through your fingers, and then pinch it off again before you begin your next stroke. With practice, you'll be able to shoot line on both your forward cast and back cast to make a long delivery with minimal false casting.

You can also use your line hand to control line on the shoot to make a long accurate cast. Make the cast, allowing the line to shoot through a C formed by your index finger, middle finger, and thumb. As the fly nears your target, trap the line.

When shooting line through your fingers, make sure you do it in such a way that you create the least possible resistance. That is, during the actual shoot, no part of your hand should be in contact with the fly line. Many fly-fishers try to shoot line without actually letting go of it. Even a powerful fly cast is a very delicate creature. The slightest friction against the fly line will hinder the shoot.

Controlling the shoot with your fingers is useful when you need to make longer accurate casts, but whenever your goal is maximum distance, release the line completely.

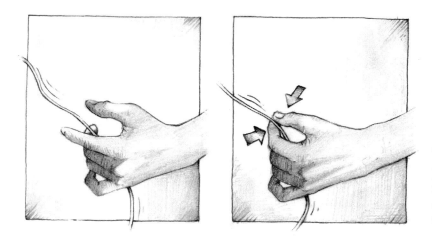

To control line on the shoot to make a long accurate cast, form a C using your index finger, middle finger, and thumb. Allow the line to shoot through the C. As the fly nears your target, trap the line.

Weight-Forward Fly Lines

Weight-forward fly lines are designed such that all the weight of the line is concentrated in the first 30 to 40-plus feet of the line, depending upon the manufacturer and the style. Nearly all weight-forward lines are composed of the following five parts:

Tip. Also called the **point**, the tip is the short section of small-diameter level fly line (usually 6 to 12 inches long) to which you attach your leader connection or butt-section.

Front Taper. Usually 6 to 12 feet in length, this tapered section of line joins the belly section and tip. As a rule, longer front tapers (8 feet and longer) are recommended when more delicate presentations are desired, as when fishing dry flies for trout or stalking spooky quarry on the flats.

Belly. Also called the **body**, the belly is the thick, level section of fly line (20 to as much as 37 feet long, depending on the design) in which most of the fly line's weight is concentrated.

Rear Taper. Most often 6 to 8 feet in length, but sometimes as short as 3 feet, the rear taper (also called the **back taper**) forms the transition between the belly section and the running line.

Running Line. Also called **shooting line**, running line is the small-diameter level line that follows the rear taper (most often, the running line and the tip are the same diameter). This lightweight length of line, which you attach to your fly-line backing, allows you to make long casts easily.

Taken together, the tip, front taper, belly, and rear taper comprise the **head section** of a weight-forward fly line. The head of the fly line contains all the effective weight of any weight-forward line and allows for the possibility of a cast that is longer than the amount of line you are holding in the air.

The major exception to the weight-forward design is the **triangle taper**. This patented design, developed by the late Lee Wulff and distributed exclu-sively by Royal Wulff Products, consists of only three parts: a single continuous front taper for the first 40 feet of line, followed by a short rear taper, which is backed by a smaller-diameter running line. The front and rear tapers serve as the line's head section. Once the rear taper is outside the rod tip, the line functions as a conventional weight-forward line. (There are also a number of specialty triangle tapers within this basic construct, such as the saltwater triangle taper, whose front taper is only 30 feet long.) The dynamics of a continuous taper—a heavier line constantly turning over a lighter, smaller-diameter line—makes for a very efficient transfer of energy.

To make your longest cast, you need to get the entire weight-forward section of fly line just outside the rod tip before making your delivery. Once you get the entire head of the fly line outside the rod tip, you can shoot yards and yards of running line for a very long cast.

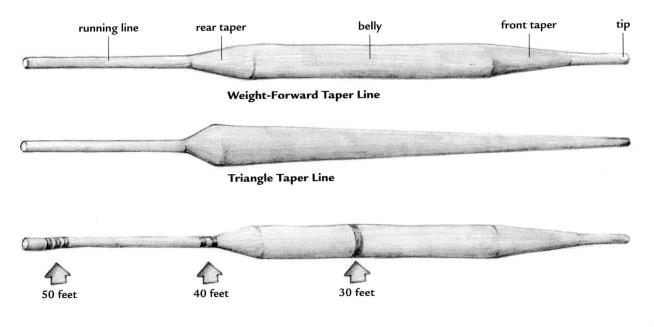

running line   **rear taper**   **belly**   **front taper**   **tip**

Weight-Forward Taper Line

Triangle Taper Line

50 feet   **40 feet**   **30 feet**

Marking Lines
for Length and Weight

Savvy anglers use waterproof ink to mark their fly lines for both length and weight.

Marking your fly lines for length offers several advantages. First, length markings will help you to make long casts consistently. For example, I mark all of my fly lines—fresh- as well as saltwater—with marks at 30, 40, and 50 feet. If the head of my fly line is 37 feet long, I know automatically that when I get my 40-foot mark just at the rod tip I'm in good position to make a long cast. If the head of my line is 43 feet long, however, I know I need to get the 40-foot mark a few feet outside the rod tip before making my long cast.

Length marks give you an accurate measure of how far you're actually casting. For example, if you make a cast that puts your 40-foot mark 2 feet outside the rod tip, you know that you've delivered the fly 60 feet (assuming you're using a 9-foot rod and a 9-foot leader).

Length markings on your fly line can also help you relocate a missed fish. Imagine you were to turn a fish in open water with no rocks, pilings, or other reference points to give you an idea of where the fish was when it made a pass at the fly. Suppose that, immediately after the fish showed, you were to take note of where one of your length marks was in relation to the rod tip or one of the guides. This information would allow you to work the fly through that same piece of water again.

To mark a fly line for length according to the method described above, use a 100-foot tape measure to measure 30 feet back from the tip of the line (not counting the butt-section or leader) and make a single inch-long bar around the entire circumference of the line. At 40 feet make two inch-long bars, and at 50 feet mark the line with three bars. Let the ink dry thoroughly before putting the line on a spool.

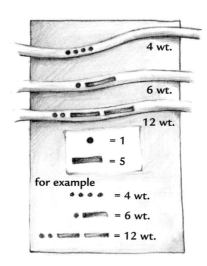

To mark a fly line for weight, use a dash to signify the number 5, and a dot to signify the number 1.

Many "waterproof" inks don't live up to their name and will bleed and smudge when wet, making a mess of your line. The best pen I've found for marking fly lines is Sanford's Rub-a-Dub laundry marker (available in the stationery section of most stores). Cut the point of the pen off flat with a razor; this gives you a much larger mark-ing surface and makes the pen easier to work with.

The above method is just one of many ways to mark a fly line for length. Choose or invent any system that is useful to you. However you decide to mark your line for length, keep it fairly simple. Also, you'll be best served if one of your marks more or less signifies the end of the head section.

If you fly-fish long enough, you'll begin to collect fly lines—boxes upon boxes of them. Wound on their storage spools, all fly lines look more or less alike. After a couple of seasons, you'll forget which is which. It helps to have a system whereby you can instantly identify the weight of a line. I prefer to mark the line in a sort of semaphore code. A dash (perhaps ¼ inch long) on the line designates the number 5, and a dot represents the number 1. So a line marked with four dots would signify a 4-weight line; one dash and one dot would signify a 6-weight, etc. When marking lines for weight, it's helpful to code them on both the forward taper (about a foot or so above the tip) and also at the rear end of the line, just above the running line-backing connection. This will prevent your having to remove a fly line from its storage spool to see what weight it is. As a matter of form, I always mark the line so that the longer dash faces the tip of the fly line; this lets me instantly distinguish the front from the rear of the line.

Casting in All Planes

Up until now we've discussed only the perfect textbook cast executed under ideal conditions. As any angler knows, however, actual fishing conditions are rarely ideal. You'll constantly be faced with impediments in the form of wind and other obstructions preventing you from delivering the ideal cast.

Casting vertically is the most accurate way to cast, and I'm convinced it's the best, fastest way to learn good fly-casting form. But once you've built a solid fly-casting foundation in the vertical plane, learning to adapt your cast to deliver a fly in all planes will give you great versatility as a fly caster and allow you to fish successfully when faced with a variety of conditions and obstacles.

A **sidearm cast**, in the horizontal plane, is useful to place a fly under overhanging trees. In salt water, this might be a mangrove. You can use a sidearm cast to pitch a bass bug under a dock, or to cast low to the water to avoid the wind (keep in mind that the wind is always moving slower close to the water).

Casting **off-vertical**, with the rod tilted slightly away from your body, keeps the fly from passing directly over your rod tip or over you and is a good way to cast a weighted fly such as a Clouser Minnow, which could break your rod if it hit it. It's also a good way to cast when accuracy isn't critical, as when fishing streamers or wet flies quartering downstream.

Out of ease, convenience, and safety, the vast majority of fly-fishers cast in the off-vertical plane to the exclusion of all others; however, doing so compromises accuracy and limits versatility. As we've said, very often pinpoint accuracy is not a concern. Nevertheless, restricting your fly cast to a single plane would be like trying to fish for every species of fish, and in all situations, with a single fly pattern.

Casting off-vertical over the opposite shoulder—called **off-shoulder** or **backhand casting**—positions the rod tip outside the line-hand side of your body and allows you to deal with a wind blowing in from your rod-arm side to avoid getting hit with the fly. It's also a good way to avoid an obstacle that might be lying directly behind your rod arm.

Casting in all planes requires only that you make slight adjustments of your forearm and elbow.

To cast sidearm, simply lower your upper arm so that the tip of your elbow is pointed at the ground or water. The palm of your rod hand will be facing the sky, and the back of your rod hand and forearm will travel nearly parallel with the ground or water during the casting sequence. When casting sidearm from a closed stance, your shoulders remain square to the target, and your elbow remains very close to the side of your body throughout the stroke. It's common for beginners, and even experienced fly-fishers, to let their elbows escape their sides when casting sidearm. However, keep in mind that the farther your rod hand gets from your body, the less strength you have. Also, the farther your elbow gets from your side during the casting stroke, the more likely you are to bring your rod hand through a curved path.

Aside from the plane in which it is executed, the sidearm cast is virtually identical to any other straight-line cast: the basics of the fly cast never change.

To cast off-vertical, raise your forearm so that it's canted away from your body just enough that the rod tip is outside the line of your rod arm. Rather than being pointed directly above you at 12 o'clock, the rod tip is pointed at 12:30 or 1 o'clock (assuming you're facing a clock; that would be 11:30 or 11 o'clock for a left-handed caster). When you're casting off-vertical properly, your upper arm and forearm will be out of alignment only slightly. Again, your shoulders remain square to the target, and the tip of your elbow will be pointed at your target.

As with the sidearm cast, the most common mistake made by fly-fishers casting off-vertically is to allow the elbow of their rod arm to escape their sides. Again, the farther away from your body your rod hand gets, the more strength it takes to cast, and the more quickly you'll become fatigued. Also, the farther from your eye your rod hand is, the less accurate your casts likely will be.

To cast off-vertical over the opposite shoulder (that is, off-shoulder or backhand), your elbow moves out from your body slightly, only a couple of inches, and your rod hand acts as the pivot point to cant the rod shaft toward the line-hand side of your body. This drops the rod tip outside the shoulder of your line hand (see illustration page 86).

When casting off-shoulder, make sure you keep the shaft of the rod, just above the cork handle, above eye level. If you drop the shaft below eye level, you'll cross your body (see photo page 86). This constricts the length of the casting stroke, and you also sacrifice accuracy. Keep the rod shaft above eye level.

If you need to lower the off-shoulder casting plane, you can move your elbow up, away from your body a little farther (see illustration next page), but again, make sure you keep the shaft of the rod above eye level. If you need to lower the casting plane more than this, do so by bending sideways at the waist. Off-shoulder, you can cast almost horizontally.

Cast sidearm by lowering your upper arm so that the tip of your elbow is pointed at the ground or water. The palm of your rod hand will be facing the sky, and the back of your rod hand and forearm will travel nearly parallel with the ground or water during the casting sequence. Your shoulders remain square to the target, and your elbow remains very close to your side.

To cast off-vertical, cant your forearm away from your body such that it's only slightly out of alignment with your upper arm and the rod tip is pointed at 12:30 or 1 o'clock (or 11:30 or 11 o'clock, for left-handed casters).

Allowing the rod shaft to cross your body constricts the length of the casting stroke and sacrifices accuracy.

To cast off-shoulder, your elbow moves out from your body only a couple of inches, and you cant the rod shaft slightly toward the line-hand side of your body, dropping the rod tip outside the shoulder of your line hand.

You can lower the casting plane further still by bending sideways at the waist.

Learn to cast in various planes first using only your rod arm, with the fly line trapped under the middle finger of your rod hand. As you become more comfortable with it you can add your line hand.

You can also roll cast off-shoulder, which you'll need to do when the wind is blowing in from the rod-arm side of your body. Move your elbow out from your body just enough to drop the rod tip just outside the shoulder of your line hand. Again, the shaft of the rod remains above eye level. Everything else about the roll cast is the same. During the stroke, your rod hand moves directly toward the target (see photos next page). If you're a right-handed caster roll casting off-shoulder, you need to make the cast to the right of the line anchored on the water.

As with all other casts, practice the off-shoulder roll cast first with just your rod arm, with the fly line trapped under the middle finger of your rod hand. When you feel comfortable with this and have achieved a good measure of proficiency, you can add the line hand.

When fishing, you'll rarely find yourself in ideal casting situations. There are always going to be obstacles. Being able to cast in all planes gives you options for overcoming these obstacles.

Learn to cast in various planes first using only your rod arm. As you become more comfortable you can add your line hand.

To roll cast off-shoulder, move your elbow out from your body just enough to drop the rod tip just outside the shoulder of your line hand.

Everything else about the roll cast is the same. During the stroke, your rod hand moves directly toward the target.

Drift and Follow-Through

If there's a single fly-casting technique that separates ordinary casters from extraordinary casters, it is the mastery of **drift** and **follow-through**.

Drift and follow-through are a repositioning of the rod after the casting stroke. You'll use them either to reposition the rod to set you up to make a longer casting stroke (that is, a wider casting arc), or you'll use them to make a cast that's in a different plane than was the previous cast.

Drift occurs after the back-cast stroke. As the length of line you hold outside the rod tip increases, you'll need to increase the length of your casting stroke. After you stop the rod on the back cast, and the loop of line is unrolling behind you, your rod hand moves backward and upward slightly. This movement of your rod hand repositions the rod tip so you can bring the rod through a wider casting arc on the forward stroke. Accelerating the rod through a wider arc causes the rod to load deeper, allowing you to handle a longer line more easily.

Follow-through is a repositioning of the rod after the forward cast. A couple of inches of follow-through with your rod hand sets you up to make a slightly longer back-cast stroke.

Drift and follow-through give the rod hand an elliptical path during the casting sequence (see illustration page 91). Rod drift is backward and upward; follow-through is forward and downward.

After you stop the rod on your delivery stroke, you'll follow through with the rod tip down to the water.

Remember that drift and follow-through occur outside the casting stroke itself and are done without force. The rod must stop, and the loop of line must be unrolling, before you can drift or follow through. If you run either drift or follow-through together with the casting stroke, you'll more than likely open the loop and destroy your

This shows the rod hand at the end of the back-cast stroke.

After you stop the rod on the back cast, and the loop of line is unrolling behind you, your rod hand drifts backward and upward slightly.

The drift move repositions the rod tip so you can bring the rod through a wider arc on the forward stroke. This allows you to handle a longer line more easily.

After you stop the rod on the forward stroke, your rod hand will follow through forward and downward. A couple of inches of follow-through with your rod hand sets you up to make a slightly longer back-cast stroke.

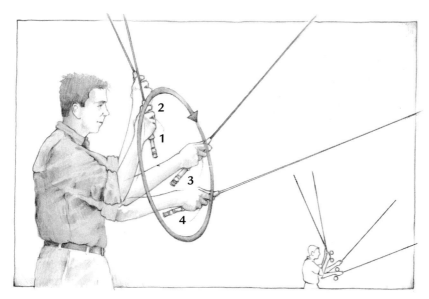

Drift and follow-through give the rod hand an elliptical path during the casting sequence. Position 1 shows the end of the back-cast stroke, and position 2 shows the end of the drift move. Position 3 shows the end of the forward stroke, and position 4 shows the follow-through.

cast. This is a common problem with fly-fishers who are first learning to drift and follow through.

Another classic problem among beginners, as well as with experienced casters, is **reverse drift** (also called **creep** or sometimes **bounce**). Reverse drift is exactly the opposite of what good rod drift should be. With reverse drift, while the back cast is unrolling, the caster repositions his rod hand *forward* rather than backward. This constricts the width of the casting arc and will prevent you from making a long cast well. Reverse drift often results in a tailing loop (discussed in lesson 2 and discussed in Rod-Arm Mechanics).

Many fly-fishers are plagued with reverse drift (also called *creep* or *bounce*). While the back cast is unrolling, the caster repositions his rod hand forward rather than backward. This constricts the width of the casting arc and will prevent you from making a long cast well.

Reverse drift sometimes appears as an anticipation of the forward cast. That is, the caster seems to get anxious and begins his forward stroke well before the back cast has had a chance to unroll. Other times, reverse drift takes the form of a forward jump or recoil of the rod tip ("bounce") after the rod stops on the back cast. Whatever the case, you must eliminate reverse drift from your cast and learn proper rod drift if you hope ever to become a good fly caster.

The amount of time it takes for your cast to unroll is called **drift time**. From the instant the rod unloads to the moment the line straightens is the total time you have to reposition the rod for the next stroke. Obviously, drift time will vary according to the length of line you have outside the rod tip, as well as the speed of the unrolling cast. Many fly-fishers, when first learning to drift, believe they have very little time to make the drift and rush through the movements, ruining the cast. Before you even attempt to add a drift move to your casting sequence, I suggest that you first make several back casts using only your rod hand (the fly line trapped under your middle finger). Simply let the back cast unroll completely and fall to the ground. Focus on how long it actually takes for the back cast to unroll. It's probably a lot more time than you had thought. As your basic casting stroke improves with practice, it will seem that you have all the time in the world to drift.

As your rod-arm mechanics progress, you can use drift to change planes during the cast. You can pick line off the water in the off-vertical plane, and as the line is unrolling behind you on the back cast, your forearm pivots to cant the rod for an off-shoulder delivery. This might be useful if you were casting in a wind that was coming in from the rod-hand side of your body. Both the off-vertical pick-up and off-shoulder delivery keep the fly well away from your body.

You can also use the same technique to make changes in direction. Rather than false casting and rotating your upper body to gradually change direction, you could use an off-shoulder delivery to angle the forward cast to your left side. This would be more efficient than false casting and is every bit as effective.

Once you learn to utilize drift time to change planes during the casting sequence, you can use virtually any combination of casts. When fishing, you'll constantly be faced with obstacles—whether it's wind, trees in your way, or a host of other things. The more versatile you become with the fly rod, and the more casts you have in your arsenal, the more options you'll have for overcoming these obstacles.

Drift and follow-through also serve several other very important functions in fly casting. Remember in lesson 3 we talked about perfect timing in fly casting being a thing of feeling. For reasons that remain mysterious, drift and follow-through help you to feel the cast unroll and enhance your feeling of being connected to the fly line.

**You can use drift to change planes during the cast. You can pick line off the
water in the off-vertical plane (1), and as the line is unrolling on the back cast
(2), your forearm pivots to cant the rod for an off-shoulder delivery (3).**

In a sense, drift and follow-through "turn up the volume" and allow
you to better "listen" to the rod. When you become more aware of
the fly line's gradually increasing pressure against the rod tip, and can
better feel the tug as the fly line straightens completely, you can more
precisely time each of your casts. *Your ability to feel the increasing pressure of the fly line against the rod tip is one of the most important skills
you'll ever develop as a fly caster.* The better you incorporate drift and
follow-through into your casting sequence, the better able you are
to feel the subtle interactions between rod and line and the minute
differences in timing, and the better fly caster you'll be. The better
my casting became, the more "connected" I felt to the fly line; the
more "connected" I felt to the fly line, the better my casting became.

Drift and follow-through also act as shock absorbers for the force
of the unrolling cast. Fly casting done without drift or follow-through
has a hard, mechanical edge to it. There's no sense of flow, and it's
not very pretty. Drift and follow-through smooth everything out and
connect each of the casts as if the entire sequence were one fluid

motion. Because of this, drift and follow-through are not skills you will use only for longer casts; indeed, they will become as much a part of every casting sequence as will loading the rod.

In my discussion on the closed stance at the end of part 1, I instructed you to stand with the foot corresponding to your rod hand about half a step back. In addition to giving you better balance, this will allow you to shift your weight from your front to your rear foot, and vice versa, during the casting sequence. Shifting your weight during the casting sequence—to the rear foot during the back-cast stroke and into drift time, and to the front foot during the forward stroke and into follow-through time—will, in itself, reposition your rod hand slightly. This may be all the drift and follow-through you need for shorter casts, but for longer casts you *are* going to have to reposition your rod hand during drift time.

When you get proficient at practicing drift and follow-through with just your rod hand at first, with the line trapped under your middle finger, you can add your line hand. At the beginning, you'll move your line hand in unison with your rod hand throughout each stroke, drift, and follow-through. As you progress, and your sense of maintaining tension on the fly line develops, you can hold your line hand lower if you wish, at about waist level. This is where my line hand is when I fish.

When you first attempt to learn them, drift and follow-through will no doubt be a very conscious, mechanical repositioning of the rod. That's OK at first, but after you work with them a while, they will become more fluid. I think of drift and follow-through as a sort of "relaxing" in the direction of the unrolling cast.

As a fly-casting instructor, I'm a staunch advocate of breaking the casting sequence down into its smallest possible increments in order to learn a new technique or to troubleshoot. When you're first learning to drift, you almost certainly will find it helpful to practice only your back cast and drift. That is, don't even make a forward cast; simply make your back cast and drift and then let your back cast straighten and fall to the ground. Once you get a good sense of the feeling of the back-cast stroke, drift, drift time, and the feeling of the unrolling fly line—and their relationship to each other—you can then add a forward cast to the sequence. When you first add a forward cast, you can follow through with the rod tip completely to the water. At this point, you'll essentially be making a pick-up-and-lay-down cast that incorporates a drift move between strokes. When you get proficient at this, you can move on to a false-casting sequence that includes drift and follow-through. That is, rather than following through to the water with your rod tip, you'll follow through only a couple of inches, keeping the line airborne and readying yourself for your next back-cast stroke.

Another good way to work on the individual steps of drift and follow-through is to incorporate them into the lawn-casting exercise from lesson 2. Although you can work on this using a short line of 12 feet or less, you'll see that as the line lengthens, you'll need to use drift and follow-through to set yourself up for a longer casting stroke to turn the longer line over.

Once they become a natural part of your casting sequence, drift and follow-through will give your casting a gracefulness that it wouldn't otherwise have. Without drift and follow-through, even a solid set of fly-casting mechanics still looks fairly mechanical. A solid casting stroke that's been polished with drift and follow-through transcends the mere mechanics of fly casting.

Off-Vertical Casting from the Open Stance

The major drawback to casting entirely from the closed stance is that it restricts the length you can drift with the rod, thus restricting the potential length of your forward stroke. When you use a closed stance and keep your shoulders square to the target throughout the casting sequence, the only place your rod hand can drift after you stop the rod on the back cast is slightly above your shoulder. The drift lengthens your forward stroke by only a few inches. By shifting your weight during the casting sequence as we described in lesson 6, you can use body motion to add another couple of inches to your stroke—but that's about it.

Although an exceptional caster can make a long cast from the closed stance, it will be easier for most fly-fishers to deliver a fly 50 feet or farther from an **open stance**. The open stance allows you to drift much farther back with the rod, affecting a much longer forward stroke. Accelerating the rod over a longer distance to load it deeper will allow you to make a long cast much more easily.

The primary difference between casting from a closed stance and casting from an open stance is that with a closed stance, your shoulders will remain square to the target throughout the entire casting sequence. When casting from an open stance, your shoulders will rotate sideways to the target during the second part of the back-cast stroke (the power-snap portion of the cast) and will rotate back square to the target during the second part of the forward stroke as well (again, the power-snap portion of the cast).

To assume an open stance, begin with your shoulders square to the target and your feet even with each other and about shoulder width apart, as you would for a closed stance. Next, take a full step back with the foot that corresponds to your rod hand (about twice the length you stepped back for the closed stance), and turn that foot outward 90 degrees from the target. This open stance is very stable

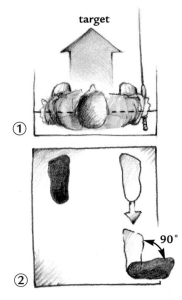

target

①

②

90°

1. To assume an open stance, begin with your shoulders square to the target and your feet even with each other and about shoulder width apart. 2. Next, take a full step back with the foot that corresponds to your rod hand and turn that foot outward 90 degrees from the target.

When you've lifted line to the line-leader connection (not shown), the loading move is complete.

and will give you good balance, and it will allow you to watch your back casts unroll (which I'm convinced is very important in the early stages of learning to cast distance). Also, as you progress, this wider stance will allow you to shift your weight more during your casting sequence, enabling you to use body movement to add significant length to your stroke. Most important, though, an open stance allows you to make your longest drifts—critical to making your longest strokes and longest casts.

Begin with about 20 feet of fly line outside the rod tip. The line should be lying on the water in front of you with all the slack removed, and the line should be trapped under the middle finger of your rod hand. When casting off-vertical from an open stance, you'll begin your back cast with your shoulders square to the target, just as you would when casting from the closed stance.

Lift the line in a loading move with the rod held 40 to 45 degrees off-vertical. The path of the rod hand is just outside the shoulder (as opposed to being in the same vertical plane as the shoulder, as it is with the pick-up-and-lay-down cast). Just as with any back cast—the fundamentals of fly casting never change—continue to lift line until you reach the line-leader connection. When you've lifted line to the line-leader connection, the loading move is complete.

At this point, your shoulders will still be square to the target. It is during the second part of the acceleration (that is, the power snap, speed-up-and-stop, or power stroke) that your shoulders will quickly rotate 90 degrees to the target, or nearly so. It is also during this stage of the acceleration that your wrist will move very quickly from bent forward to straight.

When the yarn fly leaves the water, you'll squeeze the rod very firmly and very quickly, and you'll stop the rod abruptly. At this

point, your elbow will be close enough to your side that you could grasp a dollar bill in your armpit. Your upper arm and forearm form a narrow V that's pointed at the target. The imaginary line coming off the thumbnail of your rod hand should be pointed 180 degrees directly opposite your target.

During the power-snap portion of the cast, your shoulders rotate 90 degrees to the target. When the yarn fly leaves the water, you'll stop the rod abruptly.

When you stop the rod at the end of the power snap, your upper arm and forearm form a narrow V that's pointed at the target.

The rod will unload, and if you've done everything correctly, the loop of line will unroll just outside the rod tip (see photos next page). You should be in good position to watch your loop unroll without turning your head or rotating your body (it should require only a shift of your eyes). If you cannot, that means you didn't rotate your shoulders enough during the second stage of the acceleration.

The rod will unload (1), and the loop of line will unroll just outside the rod tip (2). When the back cast straightens, you'll begin your forward stroke (3).

When the back cast straightens, you'll begin your forward stroke. Your rod hand will accelerate along the hand-target line, still in the off-vertical plane. When the thumb of your rod hand (and the shaft of the rod) is perpendicular to the target, you'll execute the power

snap, pushing forward with your thumb as you pull back with your lower fingers to stop the rod abruptly. It's during the power-snap portion of the cast that your shoulders will rotate back so that they're square to the target. If you've done everything correctly, the rod will unload, and the loop will form and unroll, turning over the leader just above your target.

During the power snap (1), you'll push forward on the rod handle with your thumb as you pull back with your lower fingers. Simultaneously, your shoulders will rotate back square to the target. The rod unloads (2), unrolling the leader and fly just above your target.

Problems with Distance

Apart from the shoulder rotation and the off-vertical plane of your forearm and rod, casting from the open stance is virtually identical to casting vertically from the closed stance. Yet fly-fishers tend to have a lot of trouble learning to cast from the open stance—even those anglers who have a decent grasp of casting from the closed stance.

In truth, you can do almost everything wrong and still get 30 feet of fly line to unroll consistently. The problems common to casting off-vertical from an open stance become most obvious when we look at long casts of more than 50 feet, for errors—and their results—become magnified: *distance casting is the ultimate test of good fly-casting form.* So let's take a close look at the individual parts of the long-cast sequence—back cast, drift, and forward cast—and the problems particular to each. Also, we'll look closely at several concepts critical to your becoming a good distance fly caster.

To practice your casting with more than 30 feet of fly line outside the rod tip, I'm convinced it's easier to cast on a lawn rather than on the water. For this you'll want to remove your yarn fly from your leader, as it may catch on the grass as you lift your line from the lawn.

Begin with 35 to 40 feet of fly line outside your rod tip. Trap the fly line under the middle finger of your rod hand. The fly line should be lying straight out in front of you on the lawn with all the slack removed, and the rod tip should be touching the ground. Your shoulders should be square to the target area. Begin with your rod arm fully extended. This will give you your most efficient back-cast stroke.

Lift the line from the lawn in a loading move with the rod held slightly off-vertical. During the stroke, your elbow will move back in toward your body, and your rod hand will move in a straight incline that's just outside the line of your shoulder.

Because you don't have the aid of the water's surface tension to tell you when you've reached the end of the first stage of the acceleration (loading move), you're going to have to estimate this. You will have reached the end of the loading move—approximately—when the tip of your fly line leaves the ground. (With practice, you'll eventually come to know automatically by feel when you've completed the first part of the stroke.)

During the second stage of the acceleration (power snap), your rod-hand continues along its inclining straight-line path; simultaneously, your wrist moves very quickly from bent forward to straight, and your shoulders rotate 90 degrees to the target.

With 35 or 40 feet of fly line outside the rod tip, you'll have to use your longest back-cast stroke. Your elbow will come back into your body until it is close enough to your side that you could trap a dollar bill in your armpit. If you do this, the structure of your arm will force your rod hand to stop abruptly and about even with your shoul-

With 35 to 40 feet of fly line outside the rod tip, you'll have to use your longest back-cast stroke. The structure of your arm forces your rod hand to stop abruptly and about even with your shoulder. This forced stop is the body block for the open stance.

der. To accentuate this positive stop, you'll squeeze the cork handle very firmly and very quickly. (As soon as you feel the rod unload you can relax your grip again.)

Bringing your rod hand up against the structure of your arm to force it to stop abruptly on the back-cast stroke is the *body block* for the open stance. Unlike the body block in the closed stance, the body block in the open stance does not cause the forearm to crash into the biceps, for in the open stance the forearm and upper arm are not aligned. In the closed stance, it is the physical crash that forces the rod to stop. In the open stance, it is the refusal of your arm to be bent back any farther that forces your rod hand to stop. Whether you're casting in the closed stance or the open stance, keep in mind that the more abruptly you can stop the rod, the more power you'll put into the cast.

At the conclusion of the back-cast stroke, your forearm is just outside your upper arm; together, they form a narrow V that faces the target. Your rod hand is close enough to your face that you could almost reach out and touch it with your chin.

If you've done everything correctly, the rod will unload, a tight loop will form just outside the rod tip, and you'll be able to watch the fly line unroll completely.

When learning how to cast from the open stance, fly-fishers tend to make several common errors with their back cast, which are discussed below.

First and foremost, keep in mind that, as with all straight-line fly casting, your rod hand must move along a straight-line path through-

At the conclusion of the back-cast stroke, your forearm and upper arm form a narrow V that faces the target. Your rod hand is very close to your face.

The rod unloads, and the loop of line unrolls just outside the rod tip.

out the entire casting stroke. In order for your rod hand to travel a straight-line path throughout the back-cast stroke, your elbow must also move along a straight-line path as it moves in toward your body. Many fly-fishers allow their elbows to swing out from their sides during the back-cast stroke, and this is perhaps the most damaging error with the back cast. If your elbow leaves your side during the back-cast stroke, it likely will move through a curved path; if your elbow moves through a curved path on the back-cast stroke, your rod hand will move through a curved path as well. At this point, even if you manage to bring your rod hand through a straight-line path through the back-cast stroke, your rod hand will still be a significant distance from your body. The farther away your rod hand is from your body during the stroke, the less power you have, and the less efficient your cast.

If your elbow leaves your side during the back-cast stroke, your rod hand likely will move through a curved path. Also, the farther away your rod hand is from your body during the stroke, the less power you have.

At the end of the back-cast stroke, your elbow should be close enough to your side that you could hold a dollar bill in your armpit, and your rod hand should be close enough to your face that you could almost reach out and touch it with your chin (see photo on page 103). If, at the end of the back stroke, you cannot hold a dollar bill in your armpit, your elbow is too far away from your body, and it's very likely that your rod hand moved through a curved path during the stroke.

Much of the trouble fly-fishers have with keeping their rod hands on a straight line when casting in the open stance is directly related to the shoulder rotation. The function of the shoulder rotation is to move your body out of the rod hand's path to accommodate a slightly longer back-cast stroke. In a sense, the shoulder rotation allows your body to "sidestep" the rod hand as it moves through the stroke (without your actually taking a step).

You must not allow the shoulder rotation to affect the straight-line path of the rod hand. That is, if the shoulder rotation moves the rod hand, your rod hand will come off its straight-line path and you'll put a decided hook into your back cast. *The back-cast stroke must be independent of the shoulder rotation.*

It's critical that you do not allow your elbow to pass the line of your body on the back-cast stroke. This, too, can bring your rod hand off its straight-line path and around a corner. Also, if your elbow passes the line of your body on the back-cast stroke, your rod hand will miss hitting the body block, and you will have to use strength to stop the rod. It helps to thrust the tip of your elbow toward your target during the power-snap portion of the cast. This ensures that your elbow doesn't go behind the line of your body and that your rod hand comes up against the body block. Notice that on a proper back-cast stroke, your rod hand is forced to stop about even with your shoulder.

Many fly-fishers, when learning to cast from the open stance, have a tendency to turn their rod hands outward during the back-cast stroke. The effect of this is much the same as if you were to allow your shoulder rotation to pull your back-cast stroke off its straight-line path (discussed above). Once again, the thumb of your rod hand functions as an aiming device for the back cast as well as the forward cast. At the end of the back-cast stroke, the line coming off your thumbnail should be pointed 180 degrees opposite your target. If you turn your rod hand outward during your back-cast stroke so that the line coming off the thumbnail of your rod hand is not pointed directly opposite your target—even if you turn your rod hand only slightly—then your cast will hook. During your practice sessions, take note of where every one of your back casts lays out. Wherever your back cast travels, it's because the line coming off your thumbnail was pointed in that direction when you stopped the rod. This is a fly-casting axiom that should be chiseled in stone: *your fly cast will travel in whatever direction you stop the rod.*

With 35 to 40 feet of fly line outside the rod tip, your back cast should unroll just above **the horizontal**—the horizontal being an imaginary line that runs off your rod tip parallel with the ground or water (see photo next page). With this much fly line outside the rod tip, you must unroll the cast slightly above the horizontal to avoid the effects of gravity; for as soon as the back cast straightens it will begin to fall. If you happen to unroll your 40-foot back cast below the horizontal, as many fly-fishers are prone to do, chances are good that your fly will hit the ground or water behind you sometime during your forward stroke.

As I've written, I'm a staunch advocate of practicing one increment of the cast at a time until you've worked out all the bugs and it

A good 40-foot back cast stops with the shaft of graphite pointed at the 1 o'clock position, and the loop of line unrolls just above the horizontal.

becomes as natural to you as breathing. I particularly advocate this for building a solid back cast, *for the back cast is the cornerstone of the entire casting sequence.* If you want to become a good distance caster, I recommend you spend at least several weeks on your lawn, as close to every day as you can manage, practicing nothing but your back cast with 35 to 40 feet of line outside the rod tip. Study the loop of each and every back cast; remember that the loop of line is your best piece of data for self-analysis. Let each back cast fall to the ground and notice where your line lays out. Did it lay out directly opposite the target, as you wanted it to, or did something else happen? To become a good fly caster you must be able to answer these questions for yourself.

You simply cannot overestimate the importance of the back cast to your entire casting game. If you improve only your back cast, your entire cast will improve dramatically. Once you've burned the proper muscle memory into your rod arm and developed a solid off-vertical back cast, once you can get 35 to 40 feet of fly line behind you in a straight line consistently, you'll have little trouble delivering a fly 60 feet with trout tackle and beyond 70 feet with saltwater tackle.

When you stop the rod against your body block in the off-vertical plane, the shaft of graphite just above the cork handle will be pointed at the 1 o'clock position. While the back cast is unrolling, you'll drift to reposition the rod tip to affect a wider arc on the forward stroke. As the back cast is unrolling (drift time), your elbow will leave your side and your rod hand will move beyond your shoulder to continue along the same straight-line path begun by your back-cast stoke; that is, your rod hand moves upward and backward on the drift. As your rod hand drifts, your palm turns upward toward the sky. The reason for this is simply because if you were to keep your thumbnail pointed directly opposite your target on the drift, it would put a fair amount of strain on your forearm.

Moving your rod hand beyond your shoulder repositions the rod so that it's now pointed beyond the 1 o'clock position. This sets you up to make a longer forward stroke. Accelerating the rod through a wider casting arc allows you to load the rod deeper to make a longer cast more easily.

The most common problem with drifting in the open stance is when the caster runs the stroke together with the drift. That is, rather than stopping the rod against the body block and allowing the rod to unload and the loop to form before he begins the drift, the caster allows his elbow to leave his side during the stroke. The rod hand is well behind the shoulder before the rod unloads. Such a stroke does not stop the rod as abruptly as it could; and because the elbow leaves the side during the stroke, it usually causes the rod hand

As the back cast is unrolling, your elbow leaves your side and your rod hand moves upward and backward. This drift move repositions the rod so that it's now pointed beyond the 1 o'clock position.

to move in a curved path, compromising the loop. On a good back-cast stroke, the rod hand comes up against the body block and is forced to stop about even with the shoulder. Only after the rod has unloaded and the loop of line has formed should the elbow leave the side and the rod hand move past the line of the shoulder.

The other major problem with drift is when the caster moves her rod hand out to the side of her body, rather than behind her shoulder, on the drift. Such a drift does not reposition the rod tip to make a wider arc on the forward stroke. If your rod hand moves to the side of your body on the drift, you will have set yourself up to make a sort of roundhouse slice on the forward stroke. During a proper drift, your rod hand always stays very close to the line of your body.

How much drift you need for any given cast depends on how far you wish to cast. Some casts require very little drift, perhaps only a couple of inches. Longer casts require a longer forward casting stroke and hence require a longer drift. This is something you must learn individually and with any given outfit—there's not really a fixed answer.

For your longest drift, you'll reach back until your forearm and upper arm form a 90-degree angle, and your upper arm and body also form a 90-degree angle. At this point, your rod will be pointed beyond the 2 o'clock position on the clock face. This will set you up to make a very long forward stroke.

Some fly-casting instructors advocate that you reach your rod arm straight behind you for your longest drift, so that the rod is parallel with the ground. I'm not a proponent of this for three reasons. First, with your rod parallel with the ground, you will not be able to feel

For your longest drift, you'll reach back until your forearm and upper arm form a 90-degree angle, and your upper arm and body also form a 90-degree angle. Your rod will be pointed beyond the 2 o'clock position on the clock face.

your back cast straighten, which is critical to the timing of your forward stroke (remember that perfect timing in fly casting is not visual, but tactile). In order to feel this tug against your rod tip, your fly rod and fly line must be at an angle to each other: they cannot form a straight line. Second, a straight arm is not a strong position in which to begin pulling the fly rod through the forward stroke. If you begin your forward stroke with a straight arm, you will not be in a strong position until you reach the 90-degree/90-degree position described above. To my mind, beginning your forward stroke with a straight arm is simply wasted movement. Third, if you begin your forward stroke with your rod parallel with the ground, you'll find it extremely difficult, if not impossible, to move the rod tip in a straight path throughout the forward stroke.

When she's drifted to the 90-degree/90-degree position, with the tip of her fly rod pointed beyond the 2 o'clock position on the clock face, a good caster is able (with saltwater tackle) to deliver a fly 80 feet consistently without hauling—which is very adequate indeed.

The instant the fly line straightens on the back cast (which you'll feel as a tug on the rod tip), you'll begin your forward stroke. Begin the stroke by bringing your elbow back close to your side as your rod hand begins to pull the rod forward through the loading move. As I've mentioned before, I regard the forward stroke as a pulling motion, particularly on a long cast, and it may help you to think of it the same way: you're pulling fly line from behind you, pulling the rod tip against the fly line's resistance, and continuously pulling the rod into a deeper and deeper bend.

During the loading move, your rod hand, which was facing upward on the drift, rotates back so that the pad of your thumb is facing directly in line with the target.

When your elbow has moved back close to your side and your rod hand is even with your shoulder, you'll begin the power-snap portion of the stroke (see top photo next page). Your rod hand will continue forward along its straight-line path as you push forward with your thumb and pull back with your lower fingers; you'll squeeze the cork handle firmly and quickly as the structure of your hand, wrist, and forearm force the rod to stop abruptly. The power-snap and stroke end at the same instant. The rod unloads, and a loop of line forms and begins to unroll toward your target (see bottom photo next page).

When learning to cast from the open stance, some students have a tendency to try to deliver the forward cast in the vertical plane; that is, they change planes during the forward stroke. Changing planes during the stroke pulls the rod tip off its straight-line path and compromises the loop. You can change planes only between strokes (that is, during drift time). To preserve the integrity of the cast, once you begin a stroke in a particular plane, you must finish the stroke in that plane as well.

When your elbow has moved back close to your side and your rod hand is even with your shoulder, you'll begin the power-snap portion of the stroke.

The rod unloads, and a loop of line forms and begins to unroll toward your target.

Virtually all fly-fishers, when first learning to cast distance, tend to use an excess of speed and power on the delivery (reasons again why I don't like the words *power* and *speed* associated with the second stage of the stroke). In fact, I've never had to instruct students to use *more* power or speed on the delivery—I've always had to tell them to use *less*.

Although we must describe the casting stroke as an acceleration, there comes a point in every student's learning where the word *acceleration* has little practical meaning and is perhaps more of a hindrance than a help. Allow me to elaborate here, for I'm convinced this is one of the great stumbling blocks encountered by every fly-fisher who hopes to become a good distance caster. When I explain to

the typical student that, to deliver a long cast, she must accelerate the rod over a wider casting arc, invariably she simply moves her rod hand more and more quickly as it travels through the stroke. The problem is that she moves her rod hand more quickly *without regard for the feeling in the rod*. I call this **casting mechanically**: going through the motions of casting without any real feeling for the interaction between rod and line. Casting mechanically results in jarring, jolting, hitting, punching, popping, or otherwise destroying the cast. This is why it's so important for you to develop the feeling of loading the rod properly—again, the most important feeling you'll ever develop as a fly caster—for it is this feeling that will govern your every stroke, whether you're making a 14-foot cast or a 94-foot cast.

Stand at the casting pool at one of the fly-fishing shows and watch people trying out rods they've never used before. The typical fly-fisher will immediately tear 60 or 70 feet of line off the reel and begin flailing away, trying to cast as far as he can. The good caster will approach it differently; she'll be much more thoughtful. Her first casts will be very short, perhaps only a few feet of fly line. Then she'll strip a couple more feet of line off the reel and try a few more casts. On every cast, this fly-fisher is "listening" to the rod, allowing it to tell her what *it* likes.

Many fly-fishers spend their lives searching for "the perfect fly rod for my style of casting." When I hear these words (and in one form or another, I hear them frequently), this tells me that the person has no range to his casting stroke: his rod hand has one speed—usually fast—and he's looking for a rod that will mask the errors that accompany a too-forceful load.

A good fly caster can cast any rod. Her stroke automatically adjusts to accommodate a particular outfit and automatically tunes in to the rod.

If you want to become a good distance caster, I suggest you forget about such things as *speed*, *power*, and *acceleration*—those are just words, and they'll likely get in your way—and focus instead on the feeling in the rod. As Mel Krieger writes in his book *The Essence of Flycasting*, "Think of casting *heavier* rather than quicker when you need more power." He's talking, of course, about the heaviness you'll feel in the rod when you've loaded it well. And that's about as good a piece of distance-casting advice as you'll ever receive.

Here I sometimes find it helpful to think of the rod as a lever. Your rod hand is at the fulcrum, and you're using your rod hand to force the end of the lever—smoothly, gradually—against the fly line's resistance to make it bend.

Fly-fishers who "muscle" their rods tend to bypass the rod's spring-flex action and use the rod instead as simply an extension of their rod arm to "throw" fly line. Again, every fly-casting stroke concludes with an abrupt stop. If you're using the rod as an extension of your arm to "throw" line, you're not going to stop the rod nearly as abruptly as you might. No matter how deeply you may load the rod during the stroke, by stopping the rod less than abruptly you'll drain a great deal of power from the cast. Also, fly casters who muscle their rods tend to form fairly open loops—a further drain of power.

To stop the rod abruptly on the forward stroke, it's critical that you learn to use the structure of your hand, wrist, and forearm. At the end of the loading move, your wrist will be in the straight position, with the butt of the rod 45 degrees from the underside of your forearm. During the second stage of the acceleration, you'll push forward on the cork handle with your thumb while pulling back with your lower fingers. The structure of your hand, wrist, and forearm will allow you to push/pull the rod handle through a 45-degree arc. When your wrist reaches the bent-forward position, the structure of your hand, wrist, and forearm will force the rod to stop abruptly; at this point, the butt of the rod will be parallel with the underside of your forearm. This structure is so effective at stopping the rod abruptly that I think of it as the *body block* for the forward stroke.

Few fly-fishers truly appreciate the effect that this positive stop (or the lack of one) has upon a fly cast. It was a great revelation to me when I learned (after more years than I care to admit) that I could cast farther not by casting harder, but simply by stopping the rod more abruptly, more crisply if you will. Once you truly learn to stop the rod abruptly on your forward stroke, you'll be able to make long casts with far less effort than you ever thought possible.

When you first learn to cast from the open stance, I suggest you use your rod arm only and trap the fly line under the middle finger of your rod hand. When you get comfortable unrolling 35 to 40 feet of fly line on both your back cast and your forward cast, you can attempt to shoot some line using the single-handed shoot we covered in lesson 4. Trap the fly line under the middle finger of your rod hand so that you have 35 to 40 feet of line outside the rod tip. Strip off an additional 5 or 6 feet of fly line and let it hang from your reel. Make your cast, and after you've stopped the rod on the forward stroke and the loop of line has formed, stick your middle finger straight out to release the line completely. If you can shoot enough line on the delivery so that you end up with 45 feet of fly line outside the rod tip, you will have delivered the fly 63 feet (assuming you're using a 9-foot rod and a 9-foot leader).

Once you become proficient using your rod hand alone to cast in the open stance, you'll need to learn to use your line hand to maintain tension on the fly line. During the casting sequence, your hands will not move in unison, as they did in the closed stance. Rather, your line hand will remain fixed during the back-cast stroke and drift. During the forward stroke, the line hand will move rearward to maintain tension on the fly line while the rod hand moves forward.

Once you become proficient at shooting 5 or 6 feet of line using a single back cast and a single forward cast, practice false casting in

Your line hand remains fixed during the back-cast stroke and drift.

During the forward stroke, your line hand will move rearward to maintain tension on the fly line while your rod hand moves forward.

the off-vertical plane. Begin with a short line, 15 or 20 feet, and gradually lengthen it. To hold 35 to 40 feet of fly line airborne while false casting will require you to drift and follow through a bit on each stroke (though ideally you will drift and follow through with shorter lengths of line as well). Then, on your final back cast, you can drift that extra distance to make a long forward delivery.

For short casts of 30 or so feet, your hand-target line actually touches the target. However, because of the effects of gravity, the hand-target line on a long cast will be somewhat above the target. Your longest delivery will unroll the fly just above the horizontal. That is, when you stop the rod on your longest delivery, the line coming off the pad of your thumb is pointed well above the target.

We've discussed using rod drift to widen your casting arc, but you can also do so by simply lengthening your forward stroke. Just make sure your rod hand stays on a straight-line path throughout the stroke, and that it stops on this straight line as well. For a very long cast, you may need to use a very long forward stroke.

Body motion will also add length to your stroke. Shifting your weight to your rear foot to lean back for a long drift, and then shifting it to your front foot during a long forward stroke, can add 12 inches or more to your stroke length. This can translate to several feet added to your casting arc. Also, any movement you enact during the forward stroke contributes to the rod's overall acceleration. Keep in mind, however, that you'll make your greatest gains as a distance caster by refining your rod-arm mechanics.

As was mentioned in lesson 4, to make your longest cast you must get the head of the fly line just outside the rod tip before you make your delivery. The amount of running line you hold between the head of the fly line and the rod tip is called **overhang**. As a general rule, you should overhang no more than 2 or 3 feet of fly line as you cast; any distance you need beyond this you should get by shooting line on the delivery. If you try to overhang more than a few feet of running line, your cast eventually will collapse. When you overhang a significant amount of running line, you're asking a very thin line to suddenly turn over a very thick, heavy head section. It's simply an inefficient transfer of power.

A very long cast requires a very long forward stroke.

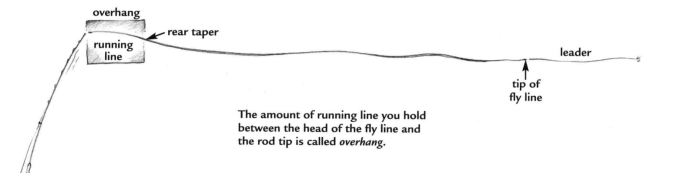

The amount of running line you hold between the head of the fly line and the rod tip is called *overhang*.

I encourage students who are just learning to cast distance to use long casting strokes with very moderate rates of acceleration, for all good casting form is learned at fairly slow speeds. Also, a moderate rate of acceleration will allow you to "listen" to the rod much better. Plow your rod hand through the stroke like a bull in a china shop and you'll feel nothing—that is, you'll be "deaf" to the rod. Eventually, as you get more proficient at making longer casts, you can begin to use slightly faster rates of acceleration—that is, a little more force applied to the rod during the stroke. Again, this is governed by feel. (Remember Mel Krieger's suggestion to think of casting heavier rather than quicker; focus not on moving your rod hand faster, but rather on making the rod bend a bit deeper.) With experience, you'll find your own best combination of stroke length, acceleration, and body movement to execute any given cast.

Hauling

Hauling is an advanced fly-casting technique. The subject of hauling doesn't really belong with a discussion of fly-casting fundamentals, and it's not something you should learn about in a basic lesson or introductory seminar. However, no work on fly casting would be complete without at least addressing it.

Hauling is known primarily as a technique used for adding distance to your cast. However, the role of hauling in distance fly casting has been greatly exaggerated and misunderstood. Although hauling will add some distance to a cast, your greatest gains in distance will come through refining your basic casting stroke: rod-arm mechanics.

Although it would be a difficult thing to measure, I would guess that a haul adds less than 10 percent distance to a good cast (and even this estimate, I think, is generous). That is, a cast that would have delivered a fly 60 feet, combined with a well-executed haul, may just break the 65-foot mark. I'd like to emphasize here that this estimate is for a *good* 60-foot cast—there is a world of difference between a good 60-foot cast and a poor 60-foot cast. For a poor cast, a haul would add significantly less than 10 percent distance, and maybe nothing at all.

On the other hand, a fly-fisher whose best cast is 60 feet without hauling can hope to add 20 or more feet to his cast simply by refining his basic casting stroke.

Although hauling is not the "secret" to distance fly casting that many anglers believe it to be, it is nevertheless a valuable casting technique that all fly-fishers can use to advantage in a variety of fishing situations.

A haul is simply a pull on the fly line during the casting stroke. Pulling fly line through the guides during the casting stroke lets you pull harder against the fly line's weight and resistance (inertia) and bend the rod a bit deeper than you could bend it with the casting stroke alone. Remember that the deeper you can bend the rod, the more power you can put into the cast. Hauling allows you to put more power into the cast with no more effort from your rod arm.

The haul coincides with the second stage of the acceleration: the power-snap portion of the cast. The haul begins at the end of the loading move, accelerates in synch with the power snap, and stops abruptly at the same instant that the rod stops.

For a **single haul** on the back cast, the line hand stops abruptly at the end of the haul and remains there, maintaining line tension throughout the delivery. The extra power the haul generates would be helpful to drive the back cast into a stiff tailwind.

When hauling, your line hand moves directly opposite your rod

Hauling allows you to load the rod deeper than you could with the casting stroke alone. This deeper load translates to more power in your cast with no more effort from your rod arm.

For a single haul on the back cast, the line hand stops abruptly at the end of the haul and remains there, maintaining line tension throughout the delivery.

hand and always in a straight line (again, think of *straight-line fly casting*). In fact, during the haul, the line hand creates a sort of mirror image of the rod hand. During the back-cast stroke, your rod hand will move upward and backward, so your line hand will haul forward and downward.

The **double haul** allows you to haul continuously throughout a false-casting sequence. To execute a double haul, you'll haul on both the back-cast stroke and the forward stroke. At the end of the back-cast stroke and haul, the line hand gives back line as the cast unrolls (see illustration next page). By giving back line, the line hand repositions itself to make another haul on each subsequent stroke. The line hand reaches a position near the reel in time to haul for the forward stroke. On the forward-cast haul, your rod hand moves forward, and your line hand moves down toward your thigh.

Many fly-fishers, when learning to double haul, give back line too

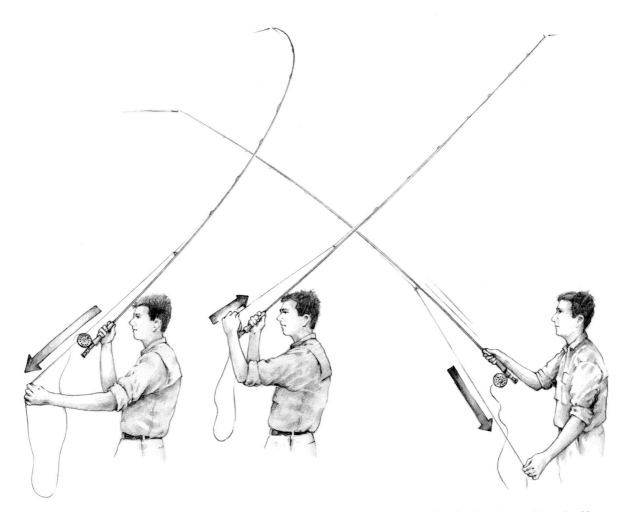

The double haul. At the end of the back-cast stroke and haul, the line hand gives back line as the cast unrolls.

The line hand repositions itself near the reel to make another haul on the forward stroke.

quickly and create slack between their line hands and the first stripping guide. You should give back line only at the speed the unrolling cast wants to take it. The haul is sharp, and the give-back is slow and deliberate.

Double hauling makes it easier for you to hold a longer line in the air during the false-casting sequence. To hold the fly line's entire head section (often 40 feet or more) outside the rod tip requires a

Hauling allows you to form a tighter loop than you could form with the casting stroke alone.

fairly long casting stroke, and the entire burden of loading the rod falls to your rod arm. Hauling divides the work of loading the rod between both of your arms and reduces the length of the casting stroke. Perhaps the greatest benefit of hauling is that *it allows you to deliver all casts with less effort.*

The other major benefit of hauling that most fly-fishers overlook is that it allows you to form a tighter loop than you could form with the casting stroke alone. Keep in mind that a tight loop is the most efficient way to transfer all the energy from the fly rod toward the target: the tighter the loop you form, the farther and faster your cast will travel. Form a tighter loop and you'll automatically add distance to your cast. I suspect that most of the extra distance we get from hauling comes simply from forming a tighter loop. Also, a tight loop is less wind-resistant than a wide loop, so hauling is critical when you have to drive a fly through a wind.

Hauling is a technique you'll eventually want to learn, but until your basic casting stroke is solid, it will do almost nothing for you. Indeed, trying to incorporate hauling into your casting sequence before your basic stroke is solid will only hurt your cast. Before you even think about hauling, develop your rod-arm mechanics. That's where you'll make your greatest gains as a fly caster.

Glossary

ACCELERATION | In practical terms, the gradual increase in speed of the rod hand and rod tip during the casting stroke. Each casting stroke should begin slowly and speed up gradually and continuously throughout the entire stroke. See pages 10–11.

ACCURACY TRIANGLE | The imaginary triangle formed by the *eye-target line* and the *hand-target line*, which meet at a point on the *target*, and also the imaginary line that runs between the eye and rod hand, which forms the base of the triangle. The narrower the accuracy triangle (that is, the shorter the base of the triangle), the more accurate your casts will tend to be. See pages 31–32.

ANCHOR | The fly line that lies on the water. See page 27.

BACK CAST | The portion of the casting sequence that unrolls the fly line behind the caster. See page 7.

BACKHAND CASTING | See *off-shoulder casting*.

BENT-FORWARD WRIST POSITION | To bend the wrist of your rod hand forward by pushing on the cork handle with your thumb as far as you can go while pulling back on the handle with your lower fingers. The bent-forward wrist position brings the rod butt parallel with the underside of your forearm. See pages 19–20.

BODY BLOCK | The use of the structure of your rod arm to force the rod to stop abruptly at the end of the *back-cast* stroke. See pages 59, 103.

CASTING ARC | The entire arc described by the rod during the casting stroke. In practical terms, the distance the rod tip moves during the stroke. See pages 7, 8.

CASTING MECHANICALLY | Going through the motions of casting without any real feeling for the interaction between the fly rod and fly line. See page 111.

CLOSED STANCE | The primary requirement of the closed stance is that your shoulders remain square to the target throughout the entire casting sequence. See page 23.

CREEP | See *reverse drift*.

CROSS-LOOP | See *tailing loop*.

DOUBLE HAUL | To haul on both the back-cast stroke and the forward stroke of a casting sequence. After each stroke and haul, the line hand gives back the hauled line as the cast unrolls (as opposed to maintaining its position where the haul ended, as in the single haul); the line hand finishes at a position near the reel in preparation for the next haul. The double haul allows you to haul continuously during a false-casting sequence. See pages 119–21.

DRIFT | A repositioning of the rod after the conclusion of the *back-cast* stroke. See pages 89–95.

DRIFT TIME	The amount of time between when the rod has unloaded to when the cast has unrolled completely. It is during this time that you may reposition the rod for the subsequent cast. See page 92.
EXTENDED-FINGER GRIP	See *key grip*.
EYE-TARGET LINE	The imaginary line that runs between your eye (closest to your rod hand) and the *target* area. See pages 31–32.
FALSE CASTING	To hold the fly in the air for more than two strokes (e.g., to shake water from a dry fly). See page 65.
FLY-ROD MECHANICS	How the fly rod and fly line interact to execute the cast. See pages 7–14.
FOLLOW-THROUGH	A repositioning of the rod after the conclusion of the forward stroke. See pages 89–95.
FORWARD CAST	The portion of the casting sequence that unrolls the fly line in front of the caster. See page 7.
GRIP #1	See *key grip*.
HANDSHAKE GRIP	See *key grip*.
HAND-TARGET LINE	The imaginary line that runs between your rod hand and the *target* area. See page 32.
HAUL	To pull on the fly line with the line hand during the casting stroke. The primary function of hauling is to load the rod deeper than you could with the casting stroke alone. See pages 117–21.
THE HORIZONTAL	An imaginary line coming off the rod tip and running parallel with the ground or water. See page 57.
KEY GRIP	The recommended grip detailed in part 1, so named because it is similar to how you would hold a key to turn it in a lock. See pages 16–19.
LOADING MOVE	The first stage of the *acceleration*. The loading move gets the rod, line, leader, and fly moving as a unit and begins the *loading* or bending of the rod. See page 42.
LOADING THE ROD	The gradual bending of the fly rod, from the tip downward (due to the weight and inertia of the fly line), during the casting stroke. See page 9.
NONLOOP	A loop so large that, for all intents and purposes, it is not considered a loop. See page 14.
OFF-SHOULDER CASTING	Casting with the rod tip outside the line-hand side of your body. Also called "backhand casting." See pages 83–84.
OFF-VERTICAL	Any rod position outside the *vertical plane*. See page 83.
OPEN STANCE	The stance in which the cast begins with your shoulders square to the

target. During the second stage of the *acceleration*, your shoulders will rotate 90 degrees from the target. In the open stance, the rear foot is typically placed farther behind the forward foot than it is in the *closed stance.* See pages 97–98.

OVERHANG The amount of running line between the head of the fly line and the rod tip. See page 114.

PICK-UP-AND-LAY-DOWN CAST The basic two-stroke fly cast that forms the foundation of all fly casting. In short, the fly is picked off the water on the *back cast* and delivered with the following forward stroke. See pages 41–63.

POSITIVE STOP The abrupt stop at the conclusion of the casting stroke that triggers the spring-flex action of the rod. See page 11.

POWER SNAP The second stage of the *acceleration*, whose function it is to complete the *loading* of the rod and to stop the rod abruptly to unload it. It is during the power-snap portion of the cast that the wrist changes position. Also called the "power stroke" and the "speed-up-and-stop." See page 42.

POWER STROKE See *power snap.*

PRELOAD The slight bend that is put into the rod by the force of a cast that has unrolled completely. See page 76.

REVERSE DRIFT The error in which the caster begins to move the rod through the forward stroke well before the *back cast* has unrolled. Reverse drift reduces the width of the potential *casting arc* and is often responsible for *tailing loops.* Reverse drift is also called "creep," or sometimes "bounce." See pages 91–92.

ROD-ARM MECHANICS All the fly-casting mechanics that pertain to the caster's rod-arm: hand, wrist, forearm, and upper arm. See pages 15–22.

ROLL CAST The one fly cast that can be executed without a *back cast.* See pages 27–40.

ROLL PICK-UP A roll cast used to pick a slack fly line off the water. The caster makes a roll cast that is aimed well above the water. Then before the cast has had a chance to unroll completely, the caster immediately executes a back-cast stroke. See pages 38–40.

SHOOTING LINE To increase the length of your cast by releasing additional fly line on the delivery. See page 75.

SIDEARM CAST A horizontal cast in which the rod is held nearly parallel to the ground or water. The sidearm cast unrolls the fly line very close to the water and is effective for delivering a fly under obstacles (such as overhanging trees) or for avoiding wind. See page 83.

SINGLE HAUL To *haul* either on the *back cast* or on the *forward cast.* When executing a single haul on the back cast, the line hand maintains its position at the end of the haul (rather than giving back the hauled line, as in the *double haul*) and maintains tension on the fly line during the delivery. See pages 118–19.

SPEED-UP-AND-STOP See *power snap*.

STRAIGHT-LINE FLY CASTING The method of fly casting in which the rod hand and rod tip describe a straight-line path throughout the entire casting stroke (as opposed to curved-line methods such as *oval casting*, in which the rod hand and rod tip describe a curved line during the second stage of the stroke). See page 22.

STRAIGHT-LINE PATH The path described by the rod hand and rod tip during a good casting stroke. See pages 13–14.

STRAIGHT WRIST POSITION To position the wrist of the rod hand such that the butt of the rod is at a 45-degree angle to the underside of the forearm. See pages 20–21.

STROKE LENGTH The distance the rod hand moves during the casting stroke. See page 7.

TAILING LOOP A casting error in which the rod tip unloads above, rather than below, the path of the following fly line, producing a loop whose legs are crossed rather than open-ended. Also called a "cross-loop." Tailing loops can result in *wind knots* tied in the leader or even sometimes the fly line. See page 14.

TARGET The desired destination of your fly. See pages 12–13.

TIGHT LOOP The narrow U or V shape the line takes on during a good fly cast. See pages 12–14.

UNLOADING THE ROD To force the rod out of its bend by stopping it abruptly. This unbending of the rod transfers all the potential power from the loaded rod into the fly line. See page 9.

VERTICAL PLANE The casting plane in which your forearm and rod arm are held perpendicular to the ground, and your loop of line passes directly over the rod tip. See page 51.

WIDE LOOP The less-desirable shape—a fairly wide U—the line takes on during a poor fly cast. See page 13.

WIND KNOT An unintentional knot tied in the leader or fly line, most often the direct result of a *tailing loop*. See page 14.

Reading and Viewing for the Student of Fly Casting

The value of good instructional books and videos, weighed against their cost, never ceases to astound me. For a nominal fee, an acknowledged authority will come into your home (via your television or the printed word) and instruct you in his or her field of expertise. For less than the price of a fly line, Joan Wulff or Mel Krieger will show you how to use a fly rod. Think about that for a minute!

Although I believe a student of fly casting should read and watch anything she can get her hands on that deals with the subject, the fly-casting works I've listed below have been the most influential in my own development—and I've also listed one of my own works, as well. Bear in mind that video can show you a good cast, but you need a book to truly explain how it's done. One thing is certain: the more you know about fly casting, the more you can learn about fly casting.

The Essence of Flycasting (book). Mel Krieger, 1987. Club Pacific.

The Essence of Flycasting (video). Mel Krieger. Club Pacific.

The Essence of Flycasting II: Advance Flycasting (video). Mel Krieger. Club Pacific.

The Joan & Lee Wulff School of Fly Casting (video). Joan and Lee Wulff. A Lee Wulff Production.

Joan Wulff's Dynamics of Fly Casting: From Solid Basics to Advanced Techniques (video). Joan Wulff. Miracle Productions.

Joan Wulff's Fly-Casting Accuracy (book). Joan Wulff, 1997. Lyons & Burford.

Joan Wulff's Fly Casting Techniques (book). Joan Wulff, 1987. Lyons & Burford.

Saltwater Fly-Casting: 10 Steps to Distance and Power: A Video Fly-Casting Program with George V. Roberts Jr. (video and manual). George V. Roberts Jr. White Mouse Productions, http://whitemouseflyfishing.com/.

Troubleshooting Common Casting Problems

PROBLEM	*CAUSE(S)*	*SOLUTIONS*
Loop Formation		
Large loop or nonloop.	Moving rod hand, and hence rod tip, in a curved or convex path rather than a straight-line path.	Move rod hand along a straight line *(pp. 13, 14, 20–22, 36, 37, 46, 51–55, 59–61, 68, 103–5).*
Tailing loop or cross-loop.	Moving the rod tip in a concave path; the rod unloads above, rather than below, the path of the following fly line.	Smooth out the casting stroke. Make sure the stroke is long enough to accommodate the length of fly line *(pp. 14, 21, 56, 57, 91).*
"Wind knots" in leader or fly line.	Tailing loops cause wind knots. *See above.*	
Pain and Fatigue		
Rod hand aches or is fatigued.	Gripping the rod handle too tightly.	Relax. Gently wrap fingers around cork *(p. 19).*
Rod arm fatigued or hurts (perhaps particularly in the shoulder).	Casting with elbow and rod hand held well out to the side of your body, placing the workload on the shoulder muscles rather than on the biceps and triceps.	Keep elbow close to side, except when casting off-shoulder, or when drifting in the open stance *(pp. 51, 84–88, 92–93, 103–8).*
Roll Cast		
Line catches around your rod tip or shoulder.	Holding rod completely vertical.	Cant rod outward slightly *(pp. 29–31, 35).*
Loop crosses itself, tangling the line.	Casting to the right of the anchor *(right-handed caster).*	Aim cast to the left of the anchor *(p. 30).*
Failure to anchor fly line on water.	Popping the fly line off the water on the set-up.	Raise rod slowly on the set-up and wait for line to slide back and belly behind the rod *(pp. 35–36).*
Loop of line has no power. Fails to turn over leader and fly.	Failure to accelerate rod or to stop rod abruptly.	Start stroke slowly, speed up gradually, and stop rod abruptly *(p. 36).*
Large loop. Very often piles up line and leader short of reaching the target.	Moving your rod hand, and hence rod tip, in a curved or convex path rather than a straight-line path.	Move your rod hand along a straight line *(pp. 36–38).*
Line lays out to the left of your target (right-handed caster).	Rod hand slices across your body during casting stroke.	Keep rod hand outside the line of your body throughout casting stroke. Rod hand moves directly to target *(p. 38).*

PROBLEM	CAUSE(S)	SOLUTIONS
Pick-Up-and-Lay-Down Cast		
Fly line rips off the water.	Lifting line with too much speed or force.	Begin the lift slowly, then speed up gradually *(pp. 48–49)*.
When lifting line off the water, the fly line slides toward you and sags.	Lifting line too slowly.	OK to begin the lift slowly, but you must continue to speed up *(pp. 48–49)*.
Large loop on back cast, or dumping back cast into ground or water.	Broken wrist.	Use limited wrist movement. Stroke should finish with rod butt no more than 45 degrees from underside of forearm *(pp. 52–53)*.
Line not laying out completely, often landing in a pile short of reaching the target.	Beginning forward stroke too soon.	Allow back cast to straighten completely before beginning the stroke *(p. 53)*.
Fly hits ground or ticks water behind you during forward stroke.	Waiting too long to begin forward stroke.	Begin forward stroke the instant the fly line straightens on back cast *(p. 53)*.
Large loop on forward cast.	Curved path of the rod hand.	Move rod hand along a straight line *(pp. 54–55)*.
Fly line bounces back on forward cast and lands on water with a lot of slack.	Too much force on forward stroke.	Use less force—just enough to get leader to turn over crisply *(pp. 56–57)*.
False Casting		
Casting sequence has a clunky feel or appearance.	Waiting until each cast has unrolled completely before beginning each stroke.	Begin each stroke just before previous cast has unrolled completely, bringing leader and fly through a smooth change of direction *(p. 67)*.
Fly hits ground or ticks water during casting sequence.	Waiting until each cast has unrolled completely and begun to fall before beginning stroke.	Begin each stroke just before previous cast has unrolled completely *(pp. 67–68)*.
Difficulty holding length of line airborne. Casting sequence often collapses.	Poor timing. Beginning each stroke before enough fly line has unrolled.	Allow each cast to unroll almost completely before beginning stroke *(pp. 67–68)*. Focus on rhythm.
Shooting Line/Distance		
Cast collapses and virtually no line is shot.	Releasing line during the stroke.	Wait until after rod has unloaded completely and loop has formed before releasing line. Use loop as visual cue *(p. 77)*.

PROBLEM	*CAUSE(S)*	*SOLUTIONS*

Shooting Line/Distance (continued)

Loop is much larger on delivery than for false casts, reducing the amount of line shot.	Overpowering delivery to get more distance, ripping loop open.	Use same power on delivery as on false casts. Focus on good form and tight loops *(pp. 77–79).*

Off-Vertical Casting (Open Stance)

Large loop on back cast. A poor back cast will compromise the forward cast.	Rod hand moves in a curved path.	Move elbow in toward body on back-cast stroke. Stroke should end with elbow very close to side and rod hand fairly close to face *(pp. 103–5).*
Hook in back cast. Back cast does not unroll directly opposite target.	Rod hand turns outward during back-cast stroke.	Check thumbnail of rod hand at end of stroke. Should be pointed 180 degrees directly opposite target *(pp. 104–5).*
Fly ticks ground or water during forward stroke.	Probably due to the effects of gravity.	Unroll back cast higher—just above horizontal *(pp. 105–6).*

Direction/Missing Target

Line, leader, and fly crash into water short of target.	Aim was too low.	Use pad of thumb as an aiming device and move it directly to target *(pp. 34, 37, 54–55).*
Fly doesn't make it all the way to target.	Probably beginning forward stroke too soon.	Allow back cast to straighten completely before beginning the stroke *(p. 53).*
Fly lands significantly to right of target (right-hand caster).	Pad of thumb pointed to the right of target at end of stroke.	Move rod hand in a straight line directly to target. Rod should stop with pad of thumb directly in line with target *(pp. 34, 37, 47).*
Fly lands significantly to left of target (right-hand caster).	Rod hand slices across your body during casting stroke.	Keep rod hand outside the line of your body throughout casting stroke. Rod hand moves directly to target *(p. 38).* Note: Same principle applies to roll cast as well as overhead casts.
Fly goes beyond target.	Fly line is too long.	Strip in line until you have the proper length.

PROBLEM	CAUSE(S)	SOLUTIONS
Wind		
Wind coming in from rod-arm side makes roll casting difficult. Line keeps blowing into body, and anchor keeps blowing to the left.		Use off-shoulder roll cast *(pp. 87–88)*.
Wind coming in from rod-arm side blows line, leader, and fly into body.		Use off-shoulder or backhand cast *(pp. 84, 86–87)*.
When you roll cast, a headwind blows your fly back at you.		Unroll your cast on the water, beneath the wind *(pp. 38–40)*.
When you cast overhead, a headwind blows fly back at you.		Use horizontal or sidearm cast to cast lower to water where wind is moving slower *(pp. 84–85)*.
Fly keeps getting caught in trees behind you.		Use roll cast *(lesson 1)*.

Index